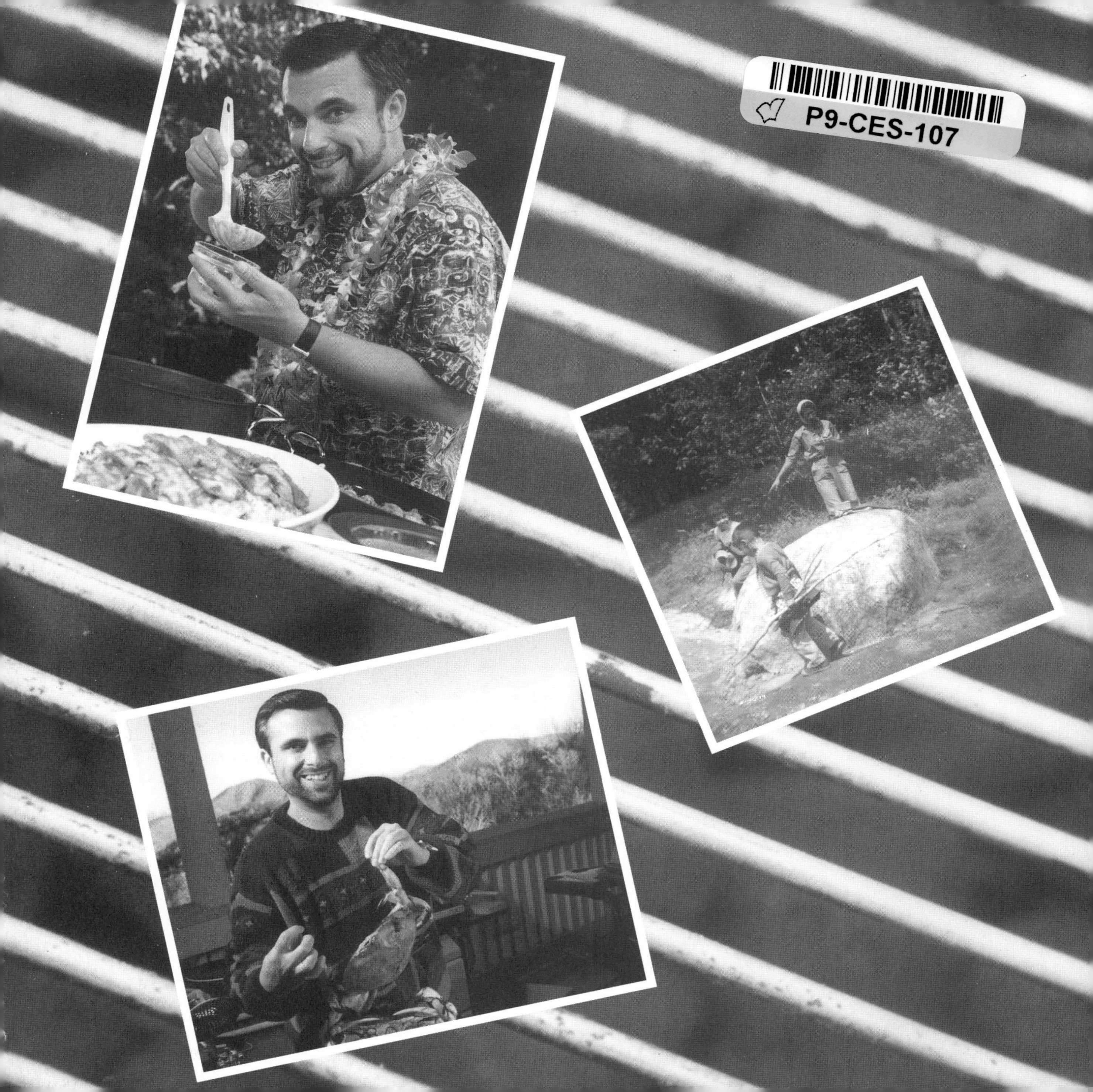

# Gather 'Round the Grill

# Gather

### A YEAR OF

# 'Round

### CELEBRATIONS

# the Grill

# George Hirsch

*with Marie Bianco*

Hearst Books / New York

Dedicated to the memory of George J. Hirsch

Library of Congress Cataloging-in-Publication Data

Hirsch, George.
    Gather 'round the grill : a year of celebrations / by George Hirsch
with Marie Bianco.
      p.   cm.
    Includes index.
    ISBN 0-688-14225-7
    1. Barbecue cookery.   2. Menus.   I. Bianco, Marie.   II. Title.
TX840.B3H558  1995
641.5'784—dc20                                  94-44619
                                                   CIP

Printed in the United States of America

2 3 4 5 6 7 8 9 10

BOOK DESIGN BY RICHARD ORIOLO

# Acknowledgments

**W**here's George cooking today? has been heard a lot around our house during these past few months. When I started Project Number Two (this book), it didn't get any easier, it just got better! But the passing of my father, my best friend and partner, made it a lot tougher.

So I'd like to thank my family and the "grill team" for their love and support, especially during this time:

To Mickey and Louie—for always being there

To Diane, Celine, and Tom—we have the best

To Dori, who always tops the list

And to Joann, the executive producer in my life, who brings all of this together.

And then there's the team:

My thanks to:

Marie Bianco, for making it possible to keep on pushing when that next deadline arrived (maybe it had something to do with the ol' picture you're looking for).

Arlene, I've always said that each day would be a new adventure with exciting places. Perhaps someday you can return and see something besides the kitchen!!

The Jacksonville foodies, who proved it tasted even better than it looked.

Dan—okay, okay, I never met a golf ball I couldn't lose.

Hey, Carol, Jack, Norm, and Steve, no trespassing when the camera lights go on.

All the people who make those great Charbroil grills. I've cooked in foreign countries, big cities, small towns, riverbanks, mountains, deserts, rooftops, and even backyards, and it's a comfort to know that when I check into a Hilton hotel, there will be a chocolate on my pillow and a Charbroil grill waiting for me.

Joe at Hickory Specialties, who knows just about everything when it comes to the wonderful flavor of wood smoke. You've reminded me of what my parents taught me when I was very young.

David, my mentor and good friend.

Megan Newman and my friends at Hearst Books, who always have a good word.

To chefs everywhere and, especially, to backyard cooks—I offer you more ideas so that you may "know your fire."

Mentioning everyone who supported and impacted on the grill team is more difficult than creating new and interesting recipes. However, I found the most inspired words written by co-author Marie, and this says it all.

We were at a cooking demonstration and book signing and there wasn't an empty seat in the house. As I finished signing copies of our first co-authored grill book, *Grilling with Chef George Hirsch*, with my usual "Best Wishes and Happy Grilling," I passed the books over to Marie to sign. When the crowd left, I finally had a chance to ask her what she was writing. It was a simple greeting—two words. At first it made me smile, and then I laughed. It sums up what goes into any creative process.

So to all those mentioned here and, more important, to those not mentioned, I quote from Marie Bianco as I write: Thanks from "Me, too."

*Acknowledgments*

# C o n t e n t s

# Introduction

**G**athering around the table, breaking bread, meeting and eating—the ritual of sharing food with family, friends, and even strangers to celebrate the good life. We nourish body and soul when we eat with others, be it a celebration of friendship, a holiday, a special occasion.

Grilling is no longer an exclusive summer sport. As I've traveled across the country, I've seen folks grilling in their backyards in the middle of a snowstorm, and I've met those who attach their grills to the hitches on their motor homes so that the grills go where they go. The grill has become the modern-day hearth where all types of food can be prepared for feasting, so start thinking of your grill as your outdoor kitchen.

Kitchen space is limited, and indoors there are just so many people who can watch the cook at work. But outdoors there's a natural curiosity to find out what's causing those wonderful aromas. And that's where people congregate—round the grill. It's all about sharing food together and doing it throughout the year, regardless of where you are and what kind of food you're grilling.

While filming the second television series *Gather 'Round the Grill* and cooking the recipes from this book, we traveled around the country to a variety of sites, hoping to illustrate how people celebrate throughout the year. From a riverbank in Georgia to the ocean shore in Hawaii to the frozen snow of North Carolina, each and every show was a celebration of food, people, and places.

We started out with the notion that once you've learned to "know your fire," grilling will never be the same. It's easy, it's fast, and it's fun—and anyone can be a great outdoor cook. So get that fire going and let's start grilling!

*Introduction*

# A Few Thoughts About Grilling

**W**ith a few basic guidelines (and this book, of course), you can graduate from making your famous hamburger à la maison to becoming a backyard chef preparing dishes such as Mole Poblano, Tuscan Artichoke Pie, and Chicken Florentine.

Grilling is not a one-season cooking technique anymore, so don't pack your grill away as soon as the leaves begin to fall. Consider your grill as an extension of your indoor stovetop or oven, capable of roasting, baking, boiling, sautéing, and steaming as well as grilling.

If you live in an apartment or condo where it's illegal to light a grill on your terrace or deck, you can still enjoy cooking out-of-doors. Pack the food into a cooler and drive to a park where there are public outdoor grills, or cook these recipes on your stovetop or under the broiler. Since many of these recipes were developed from dishes prepared in restaurant kitchens, they can be brought back indoors. Unfortunately, you'll lose the appeal of an open fire.

A menu is only a guide. Consider the season of the year, the availability of foods, and your own tastes. How many times have you decided on a certain food for your main course, but when you got to the market, the price was so high it was no longer appealing? Be flexible. Buy what's on special.

Cooking is not a science, it's a creative process. You should be in the mood not only for meat, fish, or chicken but also for the style you want—Italian, Southwest, German, or maybe French.

When you're entertaining guests, consider their tastes and health restrictions. Don't serve beef and cream to someone with a cholesterol problem (cook fish) or a sweet dessert to a diabetic (serve fruit). Plan simple recipes that can be done without a lot of fuss, especially if your guests need time or attention—such as the night you invite your boss to dinner.

And should your boss show up, make sure you ask for his or her secret marinade recipe and then share one from this book. Tell 'em it's an old family recipe handed down from the Pilgrims. It's okay, especially if you get the raise.

Decide when to begin your cooking by going backward: How long the food takes to cook, how long it needs to be marinated, and how much time it takes to get the fire going. Get organized. Are the tongs and spatula handy? Are the hot mitts nearby? Do you have an extra tank of propane? Extra charcoal?

No one should be a spectator. This book gives menus for every occasion, event, place, and holiday. Put the old adage "no work, no food" to good use. Even children can get into the act. I began my grilling career by looking for firewood at the tender age of five. A child can toss the salad, stir the dip, even lick the spoon. Guests can help by chopping vegetables, bringing food out from the kitchen, or even removing the puree from the caramelized garlic—surely a conversation starter.

The best chefs in the world know the importance of prep, the art of preparing as many things as you can in advance before you actually begin to cook. A good example of this is Chinese cuisine, and the fastest cooking style in the world is stir-frying. All the food is sliced and chopped really small, and at the last moment, just before eating, the food is cooked. Caramelized garlic, marinades, seasoning rubs, sauces, soups, and dressings should all be made beforehand; they only improve with age.

# A Few Words from the Chef

## Get to Know What You're Eating

Get used to buying only the freshest seafood, meat, and vegetables—the results will be worth it. Use foods that are natural. Learn to read labels, and avoid any with words you can't pronounce. Use natural fuels like propane and hardwood charcoal. Avoid briquets made from sawdust and binders or charcoal impregnated with lighter fluid, which imparts an undesirable flavor to food. If you prefer grilling with gas, you can buy hardwood ceramic briquets that provide "wood flavor" to the food—no one will guess you didn't cook over hardwood.

As a chef you draw on all your senses—smell, taste, sight, touch, and sound (hear that food sizzling). But the most important sense is common sense.

# What? No Salt?

I didn't forget to add salt to most of these recipes. For many years I've used all kinds of peppers, spices, herbs, citrus and fruit juices, beers, wines, mustards, and so forth to flavor foods. When flavorings are used properly in marinades, sauces, vinaigrettes, dressings, and rubs, the natural flavors of the food are enhanced. But tastes are individual, and that's why there are saltshakers on tables.

One thing I never use is MSG because of the many side effects of this flavor enhancer, such as headaches, hot flashes, and chest pains. Keep MSG in the laboratory, not in the kitchen.

# Herbs and Spices

Looking will educate you only so far. If you're unfamiliar with an herb or a spice, give it a good smell.

Store spices in dark, tightly closed containers in a cool, dry place. Heat, light, and moisture cut their potency. And whole spices keep better than ground ones. Buy herbs and spices in small quantities that can be used in a couple of months. When you buy a new spice, write the date you bought it on the bottom so you'll know when it's time to replace it.

When adding herbs and spices to uncooked foods like salads, dressings, and marinades, set the dish aside for a few hours for the flavors to be fully released and blended.

Always buy good-quality herbs and spices. You may pay a little more, but your food will taste much better.

# Know Your Fire

When you gain experience as a backyard chef, your ability to "know your fire" will grow. There are more variables in grilling than in any other cooking technique. The sweetness of an apple or the thickness of a steak becomes a prime consideration when cooking outdoors. When is it cooked? When is it overcooked?

The outdoor temperature, the direction of the wind, the moisture in the air—all these affect cooking times. For a steak or fish fillet, your fire has to be hot and the food placed directly over the heat. A fatty duck or a large leg of lamb requires low heat and is never placed directly over the flame. The size of the food and whether or not it has a bone are other factors.

Never place food on a cold grill. The grill should always be preheated, and this includes the grate. Leaving the grill lid up or putting it down also has a decided effect on the food. An open grill allows the food to sear; a closed grill gives food a smokier flavor. Putting the lid down mimics an oven and is especially useful when baking desserts.

A fast way of stopping flare-ups is to close the grill lid. With the oxygen cut off, the flames die out.

Many food preparations require multiple heat temperatures. Just as you raise the heat to bring a pot of water to a boil, you lower the heat so that the food doesn't boil over. Lowering the heat on a gas grill is as easy as turning the knob on your stove. On a charcoal grill, you move the food to the cooler edges of the grate.

When cooking steaks or chops, turn them only once. When meat is flipped over and over again, it cools down a little each time and steams rather than reaching the proper surface temperature.

When cold smoking in a charcoal or wood smoker, allow 30 to 40 minutes for white ash to appear on the coals. Every few hours, add several new hot coals that have been lit in a separate container or grill. The ideal temperature is 195°F. When using aromatic woods or bundles of herbs, presoak them in water for about 30 minutes, shake off the excess water, and place them on the hot coals. Soaking allows the wood to smolder rather than to burn.

For hot smoking on a gas grill, preheat your grill to high, presoak the wood, and place it in an iron smoker box. Put the box in a corner on the grate, lower the grill cover, and allow the smoke to build up for 4 to 5 minutes inside the grill. The grill is now ready for hot smoking. For charcoal fires, add the soaked wood chips directly to the hot coals, lower the grill hood, and allow 4 to 5 minutes for the smoke to build.

Deep-frying is always best outdoors. You keep the odors out of the house, any greasy drips clean off the grill easily, and if the breeze is blowing the right way, your neighbors will be peeking over the fence to get a look at what they're smelling.

Use maximum caution when deep-frying. Keep the kids and pets far away, and be careful not to let oil splash over an open flame. The best way to lower food into the oil is in a basket or strainer, but if you put it in by hand, gently drop the food away from you, not toward you. The temperature should be kept at a steady 360°; this is one time a hot oil thermometer is helpful. Skim any excess crumbs or food particles out of the oil to extend its life. Never salt food before frying because salt draws moisture out of the food and into the oil. When the frying is complete, place the oil in a safe place until it's cool. If the pot handle is hot, keep an oven mitt or towel over the handle so that if people lift the pot, they won't burn their hands.

Like many other things in life, grilling is a matter of practice. When you put on your shoes this morning, you tied the laces even though you may not remember doing it. You probably struggled through it the first few times you were learning, but now you do it without any effort. So keep tying your shoes and lighting the grill, and before long you'll "know your fire."

## Safety and Health

Always place grills away from the house, play areas, and traffic paths. Never store propane indoors.

Keep children away when you're lighting the grill or at least under close supervision.

Allow sufficient time for the grill to cool down after cooking, and make sure your gas grill is cold before covering it. Never leave a charcoal or wood fire unattended after cooking.

Always shut off the gas valve when you turn off a gas grill.

Limit the amount of time a refrigerator or cooler is open in warm weather. Cold food should be stored at 38° to 40° for optimum shelf life.

Mayonnaise and other foods containing uncooked eggs should always be kept at 40° after opening and not be left out for extended periods of time in extremely warm weather. A vinaigrette dressing is a better choice for salads. Use binders such as bread, potatoes, or rice for stuffing and other foods in which you would normally use eggs.

Never use the same cutting board, knife, or utensils for preparing uncooked meat, fish, poultry, and vegetables. For instance, after you have cut up a chicken, wash the cutting board thoroughly before cutting up salad greens on it.

## Marinating

Before the dawn of refrigeration, marination was a means of preserving food.

When marinating meats, fish, and poultry, avoid using salt because the salt will draw out the juices and toughen the flesh.

Certain cuts of meats and game are marinated because the high acid content of flavored vinegars, citrus juices, papaya juice, and wine tends to tenderize them. For instance, venison, rabbit, and wild birds are tougher than their farm-raised equivalents, so they benefit from marinating. Large cuts of beef chuck, pork and veal shoulder, and lamb roasts also become more succulent when marinated.

The thicker the cut of meat, the longer the marinating time. While some steaks may require only a few hours, some roasts require days, even weeks. It may seem a long time, but I've marinated a sauerbraten for two weeks and a 12 to 14-pound beef brisket for thirty days.

When making your own marinade, assemble it a few hours ahead so that the flavors can blend. To make a marinade, mix the vinegar or juice with an oil, seasonings, herbs, and spices. It isn't necessary to chill it, but when the meat is added, refrigerate the mixture immediately. In a pinch, you can use a prepared vinaigrette salad dressing as a marinade.

To make the marinade more intense for game or lamb, heat the marinade for a few minutes, quickly chill it, then add the meat.

Marinades tenderize meats, but when used with seafood and poultry, their primary purpose is to add flavor, lubrication, and moisture during cooking. In these cases, less vinegar or juice is used because these foods are already tender; they're marinated for less time, also.

# Dry Rubs

A dry rub is a mixture of spices and herbs used as a tenderizer and flavoring agent and, like the marinades of years ago, as a preservative. As with marinades, do not add salt, since it tends to draw out moisture. Dry rubs add more intense flavor to foods, but because they contain no acid, they take longer than marinades to tenderize. The tenderizing quality of rubs comes from aging the meat in the refrigerator and from the action of various hot peppers and chilies that soften the tough meat fibers.

# Vegetables

If you've never liked vegetables, try grilling a few. You'll wake up to a whole new world of taste. Almost every vegetable can be grilled. The exposure to heat intensifies their natural sugars and makes them more delicious. And since they don't require refrigeration, they're perfect for outdoor summer eating.

Peel root vegetables such as carrots and parsnips with a back-and-forth motion. It takes half the time as stroking in one direction.

Save the peelings from onions, garlic, carrots, celery, and turnips for making vegetable stocks or add them to the water smoker pan.

While you're grilling your dinner vegetables, add a few extra to the grill. Covered with a little olive oil, they'll keep for two weeks in the refrigerator and make a quick sandwich or salad.

Always choose fresh, high-quality vegetables. Here are some buying suggestions:

**Garlic:** This comes first because it is essential to cooking from this book. Look for large heads, tight skins, and cloves that are close together and firm to the touch. Stay away from green garlic because it's bitter. You may have seen elephant or jumbo garlic with cloves three times the size of traditional ones. They make for conversation, but not much for flavor. Store garlic in a cool, dry place, not in the refrigerator.

**Peppers:** Bell peppers raised in your area will have more flavor than hothouse or imported ones. Choose firm peppers with a green stem and without wrinkled or shriveled skin. If tapped, a firm pepper will sound hollow.

**Eggplant:** Regardless of the variety, all eggplant should have firm, shiny skin with no wrinkles. Male eggplants are sweeter and contain fewer seeds (look for a tiny round circle at the blossom end). Female eggplants are slightly bitter and usually have more seeds (look for an oval mark at the blossom end).

**Mushrooms:** Fresh mushrooms should always have a smooth silky skin and be without any soft, discolored spots. Turned upside down, the gills should be closed and tight against the stem.

**Corn on the Cob:** My grandmother always used to say that you had to follow the farmer with a pot of boiling water to get the freshest corn. From the moment it's picked, the natural sugars in sweet corn begin turning to starch and the kernels lose their sweetness. Look for cobs with pale silks, with never more than a hint of brown tips. Pierce a kernel with your fingernail and you'll see in a moment if the corn is juicy or dry.

**Celery:** Victorious Greek athletes were awarded bunches of green leafy stalks rather than gold medals. Celery is from the same family as carrots and parsnips. I love celery, but I hate the strings. I like to remove them by starting at the top of the rib and pulling the strings off with a sharp paring knife.

**Onions:** Many a tear has been shed over an onion because the knife wasn't sharp. Choose onions with papery skins and never buy any that are sprouting. Onions don't like moisture, so never store them in the refrigerator.

**Tomatoes:** Whether you call them *pomme d'amour* like the French or *pomo d'oro* like the Neapolitans, just make sure you don't call those hard, thick-skinned, tasteless out-of-season things tomatoes. A tomato should taste like a tomato and not have the cottony texture associated with tomatoes picked green and "ripened" on their way to market. Plum tomatoes are best for grilling because they are firm and have lots of flesh and little water for their size.

*A Few Words from the Chef*

# Fruit

As with vegetables, most people do not think of fruit as a grillable food. And like grilled vegetables, grilled fruit will surprise you with its intense flavor and sweetness.

Rely on your nose when selecting fruit. Of course, you can taste a berry or a grape from a fruit display, but sampling a melon or pear is a little more difficult. Ripe fruit should have an aroma: a pear should smell like a pear, a pineapple should smell like a pineapple.

Think beyond the typical fruit bowl that sits on the dinner table. When you plan a meal, you choose a protein, a starch, and a vegetable. Now add a fourth—fruit in the form of a relish, a salsa, a chutney, or sliced grilled fruit as an alternative to a sauce for meat or fish.

**Melon:** Using both thumbs, press the stem end. In an unripened melon, it will feel rock hard; in a ripe melon, there should be some resistance. Also, give a melon the smell test. An easy way to remove seeds from cantaloupes, honeydews, and casabas is to drop the melon from 8 or 10 inches above onto the counter. It won't bruise the melon flesh, and when cut in half, the seeds will fall away easily.

**Bananas:** If they have green tips, place the bananas in a brown paper bag to hasten ripening. Under no conditions store them in the refrigerator.

**Pineapple:** Choose a pineapple with green leaves. There should be a little give when pressed lightly on the bottom.

**Apples:** Aroma, aroma, aroma. The best apples are bought at local orchards during the late summer and early fall. Apples should be bright-skinned, plump, and crisp looking. For short storage, use the refrigerator; for long storage, find a cool, dark, dry, well-ventilated place.

**Pears:** Once again, aroma. Pears ripen from the inside out, so if they are firm, let them ripen at room temperature until they yield to gentle pressure. Buy large firm unbruised pears, avoiding any that are rock-hard. Don't refrigerate until they're fully ripened.

# Meat

**Red meat:** Choose cuts with a marbled look because the fat is a natural tenderizer during cooking and keeps the meat moist and juicy. When red meat is grilled, most of the fat will cook off and any remaining fat can be trimmed before serving.

**Poultry:** All poultry is highly perishable, so make sure it's fresh when you buy it by checking the pull date. Examine the packaging. It shouldn't have any punctures and it shouldn't have any aroma. Look at the bone ends; the pinker they are, the fresher the chicken. If you aren't cooking the poultry immediately, store it in the coldest section of your refrigerator for up to two days. If you plan on freezing uncooked poultry, repackage it in heavy-duty freezer bag or wrap and use with six months. Once cooked, poultry can be refrigerated three to four days. Save all bones for making stock.

# Fish

The secret to successful fish grilling is to oil the grate and use intense heat. Tuna, shark, mahimahi, and swordfish have a denser structure and can stand a little abuse, but delicate fish such as salmon requires more care. The worse thing you can do to fish is to overcook it. Fish should be removed from the grill just before it's totally done because residual heat will continue to cook it.

Choosing a whole fish is easy: it should smell like the sea. Look for clear eyes, a glistening skin, and red gills. Fresh fillets should look translucent, fish steaks should look moist and meaty, and both should be set on beds of ice, not in them or puddles of water.

**Shellfish:** Fresh clams, mussels, and oysters should be alive when you buy them. Their shells should be tightly closed and they should smell sweet. Never store them in a plastic bag because they have to breathe. If not used immediately, place them in an uncovered bowl in the refrigerator. Crabs should be alive and frisky. And if you get bitten by one, you know it's fresh in more ways than one.

Spring

# M e n u   1

*Portuguese Bean Soup*

*Seafood Salad*

*Orzo with Smoked Pecans*

*New York Strip Steak with Mushrooms*

*Crepes with Grilled Fruits*

The Hawaiian Islands were visited by Captain James Cook in 1778, but at the time he called them the Sandwich Islands in honor of John Montagu, the fourth earl of Sandwich, who is said to have invented the sandwich because he was too busy at the gaming table to leave and eat in the dining room. Volcanoes may provide the fire on this island, but you won't be able to keep your guests from erupting once they sit down to this menu. Let Montagu eat his sandwich!

# Portuguese Bean Soup

Makes 6 to 8 servings

*Grill temperature*

**medium, then low**

**M**ost European settlers came to Hawaii in the late 1800s to work as plantation laborers. Among this number were Portuguese, who came not from Portugal directly but rather from Madeira and the Azores. Their plain and hearty food was a great influence on the ethnic style of Hawaiian cuisine.

8 ounces dried kidney beans

12 ounces lingüiça sausage, chorizo, or any other spicy sausage

2 smoked ham hocks

1 tablespoon olive oil

1 medium onion, thickly sliced, grilled (page 303), and chopped

2 medium carrots, peeled and chopped

2 ribs celery, chopped

Puree from 6 cloves Caramelized Garlic (page 302)

8 cups chicken stock

1 cup tomato sauce or puree

2 cups finely chopped green cabbage

1 cup diced potato

2 tablespoons chopped fresh cilantro

2 bay leaves

½ teaspoon Tabasco

*Gather 'Round the Grill*

**W**ash the kidney beans and soak overnight in 4 cups water.

16

**P**reheat the grill.

**G**rill the sausage and ham hocks until grill marks appear, about 4 to 5 minutes. Heat the olive oil in a large stockpot. Add the sausage, ham hocks, onion, carrots, celery, and garlic and cook for 3 to 5 minutes, stirring constantly, until they turn light brown. Add the chicken stock, tomato sauce or puree, and drained kidney beans and bring to a boil. Add the cabbage, potato, cilantro, bay leaves, and Tabasco and return to the boil, lower heat, and simmer 1 hour or more. The longer the soup cooks, the better the flavor. Remove meat from the ham hocks, coarsely chop, and return to the soup. Discard bay leaves. Add additional stock if the soup becomes too thick.

*Spring*
*Menu 1*

# Seafood Salad

**Makes 4 servings**

*Grill temperature*
_____
**high**

**T**his salad with a loaf of crusty bread is enough for a whole meal. Look for farmed mussels; they have less mud and gunk to clean off than the wild ones, and they only cost a few pennies more a pound.

> **1 pound calamari, cleaned and sliced into rings**
> **6 to 8 ounces medium shrimp, peeled and deveined**
> **½ pound sea scallops**
> **½ cup olive oil**
> **2 pounds mussels, scrubbed and debearded**
> **½ medium onion, thickly sliced, grilled (page 303), and chopped**
> **½ cup olives, mixed green and black, chopped**
> **2 ribs celery, diced**
> **Puree from 8 cloves Caramelized Garlic (page 302)**
> **Juice of 2 lemons**
> **8 fresh basil leaves, chopped**
> **Leaves from 2 sprigs fresh rosemary**
> **Hot red pepper flakes to taste**

*Gather 'Round the Grill*

**P**reheat the grill.

**B**rush the calamari, shrimp, and sea scallops with some of the olive oil. Place the mussels, calamari, shrimp, sea scallops, and onion on the grill and cook until the mussels open, the seafood becomes opaque, and the onion is tender. As each is cooked, remove it from the heat, taking care not to overcook.

In a large bowl combine the grilled onion, remaining olive oil, olives, celery, garlic, lemon juice, basil, rosemary, and hot red pepper flakes and mix well. Add the grilled seafood and toss lightly to combine. Refrigerate for 2 hours and serve with crusty bread.

# *Orzo with Smoked Pecans*

**Makes 4 servings**

Orzo is a good alternative to the usual potatoes and rice. This rice-shaped pasta readily absorbs sauces and can be used in soups.

*Grill temperature*

**medium**

**2 cups orzo**

**2 tablespoons olive oil**

**2 tablespoons butter**

**1 cup cubed grilled ham steak or smoked ham (page 305)**

**1 cup fresh or frozen peas**

**1 cup chicken stock**

**½ cup grilled onion (page 303), chopped**

**2 tablespoons grated Parmesan cheese**

**2 fresh sage leaves, chopped**

**Freshly ground black pepper**

**¼ cup smoked pecans**

On a stovetop, cook the orzo in boiling water until al dente. Drain, toss with 2 tablespoons olive oil and keep warm.

*Spring Menu 1*

(continued)

Preheat the grill.

Heat the butter in a medium saucepan on grill, add the orzo, ham, peas, stock, and onion. Bring to a boil and lower the heat to a simmer. Stir in the cheese and sage and cook 2 to 3 minutes. Sprinkle with the pepper and smoked pecans.

# New York Strip Steak with Mushrooms

**Makes 4 servings**

In the mid-1800s, King Kamehameha III brought flashy Mexican cowboys known as *paniolo* to Hawaii, the largest of the Hawaiian Islands, to round up the wild cattle that were ravaging the land and destroying the crops. Angus beef is still raised there today on the 225,000-acre Parker Ranch, one of America's largest privately owned ranches.

Whether you call it a shell steak, a loin steak, a strip steak, or a New York strip steak, it's still one of the premier cuts of the steer. Keep it as simple as possible.

¼ cup olive oil

2 tablespoons balsamic vinegar

2 tablespoons Dijon mustard

1 tablespoon capers, rinsed

Four 8-ounce New York strip steaks

2 large red onions, sliced ¼ inch thick and grilled (page 303)

**1 pound shiitake mushrooms, stems removed, grilled (page 303)**

**1 lemon, sliced and grilled (page 305)**

**Lemon Mustard Sauce (recipe follows)**

Combine the oil, vinegar, mustard, and capers in a shallow dish and mix well. Marinate the steaks in this mixture for 2 hours in the refrigerator.

Preheat the grill.

Place the steaks on the grill and sear 3 minutes over high heat. Turn the steaks and cook 4 additional minutes for medium-rare or move to medium heat and cook until desired doneness. Serve the steak with the grilled vegetables and Lemon Mustard Sauce.

## Lemon Mustard Sauce

### Makes about 1 cup

**Puree from 8 cloves Caramelized Garlic (page 302)**

**¼ cup Dijon mustard**

**¼ cup chopped scallions**

**Juice of 1 lemon**

**3 tablespoons olive oil**

Combine all the ingredients in a small bowl and mix well.

# Crepes with Grilled Fruits

## Makes 4 servings

*Grill temperature*

**medium-high**

**M**aking crepes is not as difficult as it may appear. Try doing a batch and by the time you get down to the bottom of the batter, you'll be an experienced crepe maker. Make them very thin and remember that they cook very fast. They can be made ahead and refrigerated or frozen for a very impressive dessert for guests.

> 1 cup all-purpose flour
>
> Pinch salt
>
> 1 cup milk
>
> 2 egg yolks, lightly beaten
>
> ½ cup heavy cream
>
> 2 tablespoons butter, cooked until slightly brown
>
> 2 to 3 drops vanilla extract
>
> 2 egg whites
>
> 1 tablespoon granulated sugar
>
> Grilled fruits (mango, pineapple, papaya, strawberries, melon; page 305)
>
> Confectioners' sugar

*Gather 'Round the Grill*

**P**lace the flour and salt in a medium bowl and slowly add the milk and egg yolks, using a whisk to avoid lumps. Stir in the cream, melted butter, and vanilla. Refrigerate 30 minutes.

**P**reheat the grill.

**R**ight before making the crepes, beat the egg whites until they form soft peaks. Gradually add the sugar and continue beating until stiff peaks form. Gently fold the beaten egg whites into the flour mixture.

**H**eat a 6-inch nonstick skillet on the grill and wipe it with melted butter. When the pan is very hot, pour in 2 tablespoons of the batter and swirl it around. Cook 1 minute, turn, and cook another minute on the other side. Remove and set aside. Continue making crepes with remaining batter.

**P**lace grilled fruits in center of each crepe, roll up, and sprinkle with confectioners' sugar.

*Spring*
*Menu 1*

# Menu 2

*Grilled Gravlax with Dill Sauce*

*Toasted Peppers*

*Cucumber and Yogurt Soup*

*Swordfish with Olive Relish*

*Toasted Marshmallows*

Do you remember your first campfire? It may have been on the beach, or perhaps at your first weekend in the woods with the Scouts. Or if you were really adventuresome, it was on a white-water rafting trip. Everyone sat cross-legged around the fire, staring at the flames, mesmerized. A marshmallow never tastes as delectable as when it's slightly scorched and perched at the end of a twig. Most of the foods on this menu can be prepared at home and packed in insulated chests, then finished at the site.

# Grilled Gravlax with Dill Sauce

**Makes 6 to 8 servings**

**G**ravlax is sugar-and-salt–cured salmon—simple to make and delicious with dark bread and a dill sauce.

> **2 tablespoons sugar**
> **1 tablespoon sea salt**
> **1 tablespoon coarsely ground black pepper**
> **1½ pounds salmon fillets, skin removed**
> **1 cup whole fresh dill sprigs**
> **2 tablespoons olive oil**
> **Dill Sauce (recipe follows)**

**I**n a small bowl combine the sugar, salt, and black pepper. Pat the mixture onto both sides of the salmon and cover with the dill sprigs. Wrap the salmon in plastic and refrigerate for 24 hours.

**P**reheat the grill.

**R**emove the dill from the salmon so that it doesn't burn. Drizzle the salmon with the olive oil and sear on grill for 30 to 45 seconds on each side. Remove and let sit for 2 minutes. Slice the salmon very thin; it should be pink inside. Serve with sauce.

# Dill Sauce

### Makes about 1 ¼ cups

1 cup mayonnaise

Juice of 1 lemon

2 tablespoons Dijon mustard

1 teaspoon coarsely chopped fresh dill

1 tablespoon capers (optional)

½ teaspoon Tabasco

Freshly ground black pepper

In a small bowl combine all ingredients and mix well.

*Spring
Menu 2*

# Toasted Peppers

## Makes 6 servings

**P**eppers lend themselves to grilling, roasting, frying, and stuffing. This recipe begins with roasted peppers that are filled with a toasted bread-crumb mixture flavored with capers, garlic, and Parmesan cheese. The combination really wakes up the flavor of the peppers. For eye appeal, choose peppers of different colors.

**6 bell peppers, assorted green, red, and yellow**
**4 tablespoons olive oil**
**Puree from 6 cloves Caramelized Garlic (page 302)**
**1 tablespoon capers, rinsed, or chopped green olives**
**1 tablespoon grated Parmesan cheese**
**1 teaspoon dried parsley**
**¼ cup bread crumbs**

**P**reheat the grill.

**W**ash the peppers, pat dry, and brush with 2 tablespoons of the oil. Place the peppers on the grill, and when they begin to char, remove and place in a medium bowl. Cover the bowl with plastic wrap and set aside for 5 minutes. Remove the skin and seeds from the peppers and cut lengthwise into 1-inch strips.

**B**utter a shallow 2-quart ovenproof casserole and lay the pepper slices evenly on the bottom. Top with the garlic, capers or olives, Parmesan cheese, parsley, and bread crumbs and drizzle with the remaining 2 tablespoons olive oil. Place the dish on the grill and bake for 5 minutes with the hood down.

# Cucumber and Yogurt Soup

## Makes 4 servings

**A**lthough the onions are grilled, this soup can be made with all raw vegetables. This is what you want to eat on the hottest summer days, when you don't want to step more than ten feet away from the pool. Make the soup in a blender, chill it, and pack it in your thermos and you have a refreshing, healthy soup wherever you are.

> **2 medium cucumbers, peeled, seeded, and sliced**
>
> **1 medium onion, thickly sliced, grilled (page 303), and chopped**
>
> **2 cups plain yogurt**
>
> **1 cup tomato juice**
>
> **Juice and zest of 1 lemon**
>
> **1 tablespoon chopped fresh dill**
>
> **Pinch ground allspice**
>
> **Freshly ground black pepper to taste**

**P**uree 1 cucumber and half the onion in a blender or food processor. Add the yogurt and process until mixed. Slowly add the tomato juice, lemon juice, and zest. Pour mixture into a bowl. Finely chop the remaining cucumber and onion and add to the soup with the dill, allspice, and black pepper. Refrigerate 1 hour before serving.

*Spring*
*Menu 2*

# Swordfish with Olive Relish

## Makes 4 servings

*Grill temperature*

**high-medium**

**S**wordfish is highly recommended for grilling because it's a firm fish that can hold up to high heat and the tomato-herb marinade only improves its flavor. The colorful olive relish gets a bit of crunch from nuts.

> 1 cup ripe tomatoes, seeded and finely chopped
>
> Juice of 2 lemons
>
> 2 tablespoons olive oil
>
> Puree from 6 cloves Caramelized Garlic (page 302)
>
> 1 tablespoon dried thyme
>
> 1 tablespoon dried mint
>
> ½ teaspoon Tabasco
>
> Freshly ground black pepper to taste
>
> Four 6-ounce swordfish steaks, cut ½ inch thick
>
> 2 tablespoons butter
>
> Olive Relish (recipe follows)

*Gather 'Round the Grill*

**I**n a shallow, nonreactive bowl combine the tomatoes, lemon juice, olive oil, garlic, thyme, mint, Tabasco, and black pepper and mix well. Marinate the swordfish steaks in this mixture, refrigerated, for 1 hour.

**P**reheat the grill.

**R**emove the swordfish steaks from the marinade and place on the grill for 4 to 5 minutes. Turn and cook an additional 4 to 5 minutes. Brush the fish occasionally with the marinade. To use the marinade as a sauce, bring it to a boil and stir in the butter. Serve with the relish.

# Olive Relish

**Makes about 2¹/₂ cups**

**1 cup pitted ripe black olives, chopped**

**¹/₂ cup grilled (page 303) and chopped red onion**

**¹/₂ cup grilled (page 302) and chopped red bell pepper**

**¹/₄ cup chopped scallions**

**¹/₄ cup pecans or walnuts, chopped**

**2 tablespoons olive oil**

**1 tablespoon balsamic vinegar**

**Puree from 4 cloves Caramelized Garlic (page 302)**

**Freshly ground black pepper to taste**

**C**ombine all the ingredients in a medium bowl and mix well. Allow flavors to blend, unrefrigerated, for 1 hour.

# Toasted Marshmallows

**Makes 6 servings (more or less)**

**T**his is one of America's most basic desserts, yet I've met quite a few people who have never toasted a marshmallow or have forgotten how to. The most important point is that you must toast your own marshmallow. Those who are more adventurous can use any or all of these with the basic recipe: melted chocolate, whipped cream, chopped nuts, graham crackers, ice cream.

> **1 large bag marshmallows**
> **6 long skewers or fondue forks**

**P**reheat the grill.

**N**o cooking instructions are given with this recipe. Use your imagination or watch the kids for instructions on how it should be done.

# Menu 3

*Savory Eggplant and Chickpea Dip*

*Shoyu Chicken*

*Grilled Sea Scallops with Broccoli and Penne*

*Mushroom Salad*

*Indian Pumpkin Griddle Cakes*

Hawaii reflects the topography of our whole nation—desert, rain forest, snow-capped mountains, waterfalls, rivers, coastlines. It's one of the few states where not only can you ski on water and snow on the same day, you can do it every day of the year. Mother Nature is very talented, and we should take advantage of the myriad of foods we have at our doorstep coming from the garden, sea, land, and air.

# Savory Eggplant and Chickpea Dip

### Makes 4 to 6 servings

*Grill temperature*

**high-medium**

**B**oth chickpeas and eggplant are Middle Eastern favorites, especially for dips. This one combines both and can be served on toasted pita bread triangles. Or you can change its ethnic boundaries and scoop it up with grilled tortillas or crusty French bread.

> **2 to 3 medium eggplants**
> **4 tablespoons olive oil**
> **One 16-ounce can chickpeas, drained**
> **Puree from 2 heads Caramelized Garlic (page 302)**
> **Juice of 1 lemon**
> **1 teaspoon chopped fresh cilantro**
> **1 teaspoon Oriental sesame oil**
> **½ teaspoon ground cumin**
> **½ teaspoon Tabasco**
> **¼ cup sour cream**
> **8 to 10 scallions, grilled (page 303) and chopped**

*Gather 'Round the Grill*

**P**reheat the grill.

**B**rush the eggplants with 2 tablespoons of the olive oil and place on grill. When the eggplants are slightly charred, 12 to 15 minutes, remove and split them open. Scrape out the pulp, discarding the seeds and skin.

**P**uree the chickpeas in a blender or food processor. Place in a medium bowl with the eggplant pulp, remaining 2 tablespoons olive oil, garlic, lemon juice, cilantro, sesame oil, cumin, and Tabasco and mix well. Stir in the sour cream and drizzle with remaining olive oil. Sprinkle on the grilled scallions.

# Shoyu Chicken

### Makes 4 servings

**S**hoyu is another name for Japanese soy sauce, made from fermented soy beans, barley, and salt. It was brought to Japan around the sixth century by Buddhist monks.

**1 cup Shoyu Marinade (recipe follows)**

**One 3-pound chicken, cut into 8 to 10 pieces**

**2 tablespoons sherry**

**2 tablespoons honey**

**1 teaspoon chopped fresh cilantro**

**1 teaspoon fresh lemon juice**

**¼ teaspoon ground allspice**

**Pinch ground nutmeg**

**P**our the shoyu marinade over the chicken and marinate in the refrigerator for 3 to 4 hours or overnight.

**P**reheat the grill.

**T**o make the basting sauce combine the sherry, honey, cilantro, lemon juice, allspice, and nutmeg in a small bowl and mix well.

**R**emove the chicken from the marinade and place on the grill, turning every 8 to 10 minutes until fully cooked, 35 to 40 minutes. After about 30 minutes of cooking, brush the chicken with the basting sauce.

*Gather 'Round the Grill*

# Shoyu Marinade

### Makes about 1 1/4 cups

½ cup Japanese soy sauce

¼ cup light or dark brown sugar

¼ cup chopped scallions

Puree from 8 cloves Caramelized Garlic (page 302)

1 tablespoon Oriental sesame oil

1 tablespoon chopped fresh ginger

1 teaspoon Tabasco

Combine all ingredients in a small bowl and stir well.

*Spring*
*Menu 3*

# Grilled Sea Scallops with Broccoli and Penne

### Makes 4 servings

*Grill temperature*

**high-medium**

**R**ather than use wooden skewers, thread these sea scallops onto rosemary stems, which impart a wonderful aroma and flavor. In case you can't get the rosemary stems, soak wooden skewers for 30 minutes in water. Grilling the broccoli gives it a smoky flavor that even George Bush would go for.

**1 pound penne**

**8 tablespoons olive oil**

**4 large, thick rosemary stems**

**1 pound sea scallops**

**½ teaspoon chili oil**

**1 cup broccoli stems, peeled, blanched, and sliced lengthwise**

**2 cups broccoli florets, blanched**

**Juice and zest of 2 lemons**

**1 cup very hot chicken stock**

**¼ cup grated Parmesan cheese**

*Gather 'Round the Grill*

**C**ook the penne on a stovetop until al dente. Place in a bowl, toss with 2 tablespoons of the olive oil, and keep warm while preparing the sauce.

**P**reheat the grill.

**U**sing the rosemary stems as skewers, thread them evenly with the scallops and marinate in a combination of 4 tablespoons olive oil and the chili oil for 15 minutes.

**B**rush the broccoli stems with the remaining 2 tablespoons olive oil and grill them and the scallops for 4 to 5 minutes. Do not overcook. Mix the broccoli florets, stems, lemon juice and zest, hot stock, and Parmesan cheese together and toss with the cooked penne. Arrange on a serving platter and place the scallop skewers on top.

# *Mushroom Salad*

**Makes 4 servings**

**A** mushroom salad served with grilled meats or seafood makes an unbeatable combination. Vegetarians might prefer the salad with olives, red ripe tomatoes, and grilled onions on a bed of lettuce. Use any type mushroom you prefer—white button, shiitake, or cremini.

**1 pound fresh mushrooms**

**4 tablespoons olive oil**

**Juice of 1 lemon**

**1 teaspoon chopped fresh cilantro**

**Freshly ground black pepper to taste**

**P**reheat the grill.

**W**ash the mushrooms quickly, if necessary, and pat dry. Discard their stems if woody. Brush the mushrooms with 2 tablespoons of the olive oil and quickly grill for 2 to 3 minutes. When the mushrooms are cooked, place in a bowl, add the remaining 2 tablespoons olive oil, lemon juice, cilantro, and black pepper and toss gently.

*Grill temperature*

**high**

*Spring Menu 3*

# Indian Pumpkin Griddle Cakes

### Makes 6 servings

*Grill temperature*

**medium**

**G**riddle cakes don't necessarily have to be morning fare, and certainly can be enjoyed after 10 o'clock in the morning. Rather than with a sugary syrup, try them topped with applesauce, slices of soft summer fruit, or nonfat frozen yogurt.

> **2 cups yellow cornmeal**
>
> **¼ cup brown sugar**
>
> **1 teaspoon baking soda**
>
> **½ teaspoon salt**
>
> **4 tablespoons butter, melted and cooked until it's light brown**
>
> **1½ cups hot milk**
>
> **1 cup canned pumpkin (not pumpkin pie mix)**
>
> **1 teaspoon vanilla extract**
>
> **½ teaspoon ground allspice**
>
> **2 eggs, lightly beaten**

**I**n a medium bowl combine the cornmeal, brown sugar, baking soda, and salt. Add the butter and hot milk and stir well. Add the pumpkin, vanilla, and allspice and mix well. Stir in the eggs and blend well.

**P**reheat the grill.

*Gather 'Round the Grill*

**C**oat a heavy skillet with vegetable cooking spray and heat on the grill. Add a large spoonful of the batter and cook until the underside is light brown, about 1 to 2 minutes. Turn the pancake and cook on the other side. Repeat until all the batter is used.

# Menu 4

*Escarole Soup*

*Niçoise Salad*

*Chicken Florentine*

*New Potatoes with Roasted Tomato Vinaigrette*

*Baked Pears*

**M**any of our backyard patios and decks have become extensions of our kitchens and dining rooms, as we find ourselves preferring to cook and eat out-of-doors. The pace is slower, and the view is nicer. So take time to appreciate those long hours spent on your hands and knees tending flowers, or think about the countless bags of leaves you've raked up and mulched. Magic happens each time you light your grill: your backyard becomes a paradise that's nice to share with others.

# Escarole Soup

## Makes 6 to 8 servings

*Grill temperature*

**medium**

**G**ood as it is, leftover Escarole Soup can have a change of character: make it hotter by adding red pepper flakes or heartier by adding some cooked pasta. You might even make Escarole Soup into a sweet-tasting lettuce soup by substituting two heads of Boston lettuce for the escarole.

1 head escarole

Olive oil

2 large onions, thickly sliced, grilled (page 303), and chopped

Puree from 2 heads Caramelized Garlic (page 302)

8 cups chicken stock

One 19-ounce can cannellini beans, drained and rinsed

2 tablespoons chopped fresh Italian parsley

2 tablespoons chopped fresh basil

1 bay leaf

½ teaspoon Tabasco

¼ cup grated Parmesan cheese

**P**reheat the grill and side burner.

*Gather 'Round the Grill*

**W**ash the escarole, brush lightly with olive oil, and grill 1 minute. Remove and chop coarsely.

**H**eat 1 tablespoon olive oil in a 4-quart pot and cook the onions and garlic on a side burner for 2 minutes. Add the chicken stock, the chopped escarole, beans, parsley, basil, bay leaf, and Tabasco. Bring the soup to a boil, lower heat, and simmer 30 to 35 minutes. Discard the bay leaf. Stir in the Parmesan cheese.

# Niçoise Salad

## Makes 4 servings

Grill
temperature
**high**

**N**içoise is the name given to dishes typical of the foods eaten in the area around Nice, in the South of France. Most often, this salad is served with canned tuna fish, but if you try it with fresh grilled tuna, you'll never go back to the old way.

To make toasted croutons, brush 2 slices of Italian or French bread with olive oil, grill on both sides until light brown, and cut into 1-inch squares.

> **1 fresh tuna steak, about 1 pound**
> **¼ cup Tuna Marinade (recipe follows)**
> **1 head romaine lettuce, quartered**
> **1 tablespoon olive oil**
> **1 cup green beans, blanched and sliced**
> **1 cup cooked white beans, such as cannellini or navy beans**
> **4 hard-cooked eggs, quartered**
> **8 plum tomatoes, split and grilled (page 303)**
> **1 cup grilled croutons**
> **½ cup Niçoise Dressing (recipe follows)**

**P**reheat the grill.

**M**arinate the tuna in the Tuna Marinade for 30 minutes. Soak the romaine in water and olive oil for a few minutes, drain, and sear on the grill for 2 minutes. Place tuna on the grill and cook 2 minutes on each side. Remove and let sit 1 minute before slicing. Arrange the romaine on a serving dish and place the green beans, white beans, hard-cooked eggs, tomatoes, and croutons on the lettuce. Place the sliced tuna in the center and cover with the dressing.

Spring
Menu 4

*(continued)*

# Tuna Marinade

**Makes about ²/₃ cup**

¼ **cup olive oil**

¼ **cup Marsala wine**

**1 tablespoon chopped fresh sage**

½ **teaspoon Dijon mustard**

**Freshly ground black pepper**

Combine all ingredients in a small bowl and mix well.

# Nicoise Dressing

**Makes about ¹/₂ cup**

¼ **cup mayonnaise**

**Juice and zest of 2 lemons**

**1 tablespoon crushed black peppercorns**

Combine all ingredients in a small bowl and mix well.

*Gather
'Round
the
Grill*

# Chicken Florentine

### Makes 4 servings

When a dish is prepared Florentine style, it means that spinach is included somewhere. The connection between Florence, Italy, and spinach has never been discovered and the Florentines don't prefer spinach any more than other Italians.

**1 cup tightly packed fresh spinach leaves, or ½ cup defrosted
   frozen spinach**
**¼ cup chopped onion**
**3 tablespoons grated Parmesan cheese**
**Puree from 8 cloves Caramelized Garlic (page 302)**
**6 fresh basil leaves, chopped**
**1 cup fresh bread crumbs**
**¼ cup mayonnaise**
**3 tablespoons olive oil**
**½ teaspoon Tabasco**
**Salt and pepper to taste**
**Eight 3- to 4-ounce chicken cutlets, pounded lightly on both sides**
**Lemon slices, for garnish**

Place the spinach in a food processor with the onion, Parmesan cheese, garlic, and basil leaves. Blend until smooth. Place the mixture in a small bowl and add the bread crumbs, mayonnaise, 1 tablespoon of the olive oil, Tabasco, salt, and pepper.

(continued)

**P**ut the chicken cutlets on a flat surface and place an equal amount of stuffing in the center of each one. Fold in the sides of the chicken cutlets; beginning at the bottom, roll them tight and secure each with a toothpick.

**P**reheat the grill.

**B**rush the chicken with some of the remaining 2 tablespoons olive oil and grill 4 to 5 minutes on each side. Use any remaining olive oil to brush the chicken occasionally. Serve with lemon slices.

## New Potatoes with Roasted Tomato Vinaigrette

**Makes 6 to 8 servings**

**N**othing is as simple as boiling a potato, but the trick to this potato salad is making the roasted tomato vinaigrette a day or two in advance, letting all those great flavors come together.

**2 to 2½ pounds new red potatoes**

**6 scallions, grilled (page 303) and cut into 1-inch pieces**

**Puree from 3 cloves Caramelized Garlic (page 302)**

**1 teaspoon dried basil**

**1 teaspoon dried parsley**

**1 teaspoon dried thyme**

**1 teaspoon Dijon mustard**

**½ teaspoon Tabasco**

**⅔ cup olive oil**

**1½ tablespoons balsamic vinegar**

**1½ tablespoons cider vinegar**

**8 plum tomatoes, split, grilled (page 303), peeled, seeded,**
    **and coarsely chopped**

Preheat the grill.

Place the potatoes in a saucepan, cover with water, and boil on a side burner or stovetop gently for 18 to 20 minutes or until tender when pierced with a paring knife. Drain, slice, and combine with the scallions in a serving bowl. In a separate bowl combine the garlic, basil, parsley, thyme, mustard, and Tabasco and mix well. Stir in the olive oil and whisk in the balsamic and cider vinegars. Pour the dressing over the potatoes and mix well. Add the tomato and toss gently.

*Spring*
*Menu 4*

# Baked Pears

### Makes 4 servings

**B**aked apples are a favorite dessert, so why not pears? Use Anjou, Bosc, or Bartlett pears that are ripe yet firm, with no soft spots.

**4 large pears**

**¼ cup (½ stick) butter or margarine**

**¼ cup dried cookie crumbs**

**2 tablespoons granulated sugar**

**2 tablespoons brown sugar**

**2 tablespoons raisins**

**2 tablespoons finely chopped nuts (walnuts, pecans, almonds
 or macadamias)**

**1 teaspoon ground cinnamon**

**Pinch ground nutmeg**

**½ cup apple juice**

**P**reheat the grill.

**H**alve and core the pears, leaving a half-inch at the bottom. (Peeling the pears is optional.) In a small bowl mix the butter, cookie crumbs, both sugars, raisins, nuts, cinnamon, and nutmeg. Pack the mixture into the pear cavities and place them in a buttered ovenproof dish that just fits them. Pour in the juice, cover with foil, and place on the grill for 15 to 20 minutes with the grill hood down. Serve warm or chilled with whipped cream or ice cream.

# Menu 5

*Fried Calamari*

*Filo Cheese Tart*

*Grilled Leeks*

*Mixed Grill and Vegetables*

*Chocolate Cupcakes*

Be it large or small, every winning occasion calls for a celebration. You've landed that big movie contract or you're watching the first home video of the new baby. You've just completed writing your first book or written a friend that letter you've been putting off. You've just received a major league baseball contract (and there's no strike) or your hometown Little League team won the championship. This is a menu for all winners—a mixed grill with a sampling of something for everyone.

# Fried Calamari

## Makes 4 servings

**Y**ou may argue that this is not a grilled dish, but there's no better place to fry foods than outdoors. This is an instance when a grill with a side burner comes in mighty handy. And with all that fresh air, fried foods taste better, too. Serve the fried calamari with lemon wedges, Grilled Tomato Sauce (page 290), Grilled Salsa (page 143), or Garlic Mayonnaise Dip (recipe follows).

**3 pounds calamari (squid), cleaned and sliced**

**2 cups milk**

**1 cup bread crumbs**

**½ cup fine yellow cornmeal**

**½ cup all-purpose flour**

**1 teaspoon dried basil**

**1 teaspoon dried parsley**

**1 teaspoon cayenne pepper**

**¼ teaspoon ground nutmeg**

**1 quart vegetable oil, for frying**

**I**n a medium bowl combine the calamari and the milk, cover, and refrigerate for 24 hours.

**P**reheat the grill or side burner.

**I**n a shallow dish combine the bread crumbs, cornmeal, flour, basil, parsley, cayenne pepper, and nutmeg and mix well. Heat the oil to 360° F. on grill or side burner. Drain the calamari and dredge in the breading mixture. Fry immediately in the hot oil and drain on paper towels.

*Gather 'Round the Grill*

# Garlic Mayonnaise Dip

**Makes about 1 cup**

**U**se as a dip with crudités, grilled bread, tortillas, or pita bread. It can also be used as a dressing for seafood.

> ½ **cup sour cream**
> ½ **cup plain yogurt or mayonnaise**
> **Puree from 1 head Caramelized Garlic (page 302)**
> **2 tablespoons grated Parmesan cheese**
> **Juice of ½ lemon**
> ½ **teaspoon paprika**
> ½ **teaspoon Tabasco**
> ½ **teaspoon dry mustard**

**I**n a small bowl combine the ingredients and chill 1 hour before serving.

# Filo Cheese Tart

### Makes 4 servings

*Grill temperature*

**medium**

**H**ere's a perfect way to clean out the refrigerator. Use a mixture of cheeses, whatever herbs you have on hand, and any grilled shrimp, chicken, ham, or mushrooms you've been saving.

**4 sheets filo pastry**

**3 tablespoons melted butter**

**2 tablespoons dry bread crumbs**

**2 cups half-and-half**

**4 eggs**

**½ teaspoon Tabasco**

**Pinch ground nutmeg**

**1 teaspoon assorted dried herbs—thyme, basil or parsley**

**1 thickly sliced onion, grilled (page 303) and diced**

**1 cup grated cheese, either Swiss or Cheddar or a mixture of both**

**P**reheat the grill.

**B**rush a sheet of the filo pastry with butter and line a 9-inch tart or pie pan. Sprinkle the buttered filo with some of the bread crumbs. Continue brushing the remaining sheets with butter, sprinkling with bread crumbs, and layering them in the tart pan. Carefully fold the excess filo hanging over the rim back into the pan. Place the tart pan on grill, lower the lid, and lightly bake for 5 minutes. Cool the shell.

**T**o make the tart filling, combine the half-and-half, eggs, Tabasco, nutmeg, and herbs. Scatter the onion and cheese in the bottom of the tart shell and cover with

*Gather 'Round the Grill*

the half-and-half mixture. Place the tart pan on a raised rack (or build one with 2 bricks placed side by side) and bake with the lid down for 35 to 40 minutes or until set. Remove the tart and let it stand 15 minutes.

# Grilled Leeks

### Makes 4 servings

**P**erhaps the only time we think of using a leek is when there's a pot of soup ready to go on the stove. As a member of the onion family, leeks do as well as onions, garlic, and scallions on the grill, but they need a good cleaning to rid them of the sand that hides in between the white leaves.

*Grill temperature*

**medium**

> **8 leeks, white part only, split and rinsed well**
> **1 cup Grilling Vinaigrette (page 111)**
> **Freshly ground black pepper**
> **Lemon wedges and mustard**

**M**arinate the leeks in the vinaigrette for a minimum of 2 hours (overnight is better).

**P**reheat the grill.

**R**emove the leeks from the marinade and grill until tender, about 10 to 12 minutes, turning and basting occasionally with the vinaigrette. Sprinkle with black pepper and serve with lemon wedges and a flavorful mustard.

*Spring Menu 5*

# Mixed Grill and Vegetables

**Makes 4 servings**

**M**ixed grill doesn't necessarily mean kidneys and steak. This one combines several marinated meats as well as a variety of vegetables. Each is marinated in its own flavorful mixture and then grilled together, so the total is more than the sum of its parts.

Of course, you can add corn on the cob and mushrooms and substitute pork chops for the lamb chops. This wholesome dish is best served with a grainy mustard and dark bread.

> **Mixed Grill Marinade (recipe follows)**
>
> **4 lamb chops (1 split rack or 2 large chops, halved)**
>
> **2 large chicken cutlets, cut into 4 pieces each**
>
> **4 spicy sausages, such as bratwurst**
>
> **1 ham steak, cut into 4 pieces**
>
> **4 russet potatoes, parboiled**
>
> **1 zucchini, cut lengthwise into 4 quarters**
>
> **4 plum tomatoes, split**
>
> **Vegetable Marinade (recipe follows)**
>
> **Puree from 4 heads Caramelized Garlic (page 302)**

**M**arinate the meats separately for 1 hour in the mixed grill marinade. In a separate bowl combine the vegetables and the vegetable marinade for 1 hour.

**P**reheat the grill.

**P**lace the lamb chops, chicken cutlets, sausage, ham steak, potatoes, zucchini, and plum tomatoes on the grill and cook until desired doneness.

Garnish each dish with a head of Caramelized Garlic to spread on the meat and vegetables.

## Mixed Grill Marinade

**Makes about ¹/₂ cup**

¼ cup olive oil

Juice of 1 lemon

1 tablespoon chopped fresh Italian parsley

½ teaspoon dry mustard

½ teaspoon Tabasco

Pinch ground allspice or nutmeg

Combine all the ingredients in a small bowl and mix well. Let sit at room temperature for 1 hour before using.

## Vegetable Marinade

**Makes about 1 cup**

¼ cup olive oil

2 tablespoons balsamic vinegar

2 tablespoons Dijon mustard

1 tablespoon honey

½ teaspoon Tabasco

Freshly ground black pepper to taste

Combine all ingredients in a small bowl and mix well.

# Chocolate Cupcakes

**Makes 10**

*Grill temperature*

**medium**

This dessert, part soufflé, part cupcake, part candy filling, is very easy to make. No need to be a French master pastry chef, but you do need to be an ardent chocolate lover.

**1¼ cups all-purpose flour**

**1⅓ cups sugar**

**⅓ cup cocoa**

**¾ teaspoon baking soda**

**½ teaspoon salt**

**1 cup milk**

**1 tablespoon distilled white vinegar**

**⅓ cup vegetable oil**

**1 egg**

**1 teaspoon vanilla extract**

**8 ounces cream cheese, at room temperature**

**2 teaspoons grated orange peel**

**¾ cup semisweet chocolate chips**

*Gather 'Round the Grill*

**P**reheat the grill.

**I**n a medium bowl combine the flour, 1 cup sugar, cocoa, baking soda, and salt and mix well.

56

Combine the milk and vinegar in a separate bowl and allow to stand 5 minutes for the milk to sour. Add the oil, egg, and vanilla and mix well.

Pour the wet ingredients into the dry ingredients and mix until just moistened. Do not overbeat.

In a small bowl combine the cream cheese, remaining ⅓ cup sugar, orange peel, and chocolate chips and mix until well blended.

Pour the batter evenly into the 4- or 6-ounce buttered ceramic ramekins or cupcake tins. Divide the cream cheese mixture into 10 equal balls and drop one into the center of each batter. Place 2 bricks side-by-side in the center of the grill grid. Place the ramekins on top, close the grill hood, and bake for 7 to 8 minutes. Remove ramekins, let stand 2 to 3 minutes, and unmold if desired, or eat right out of the ramekin.

# Menu 6

*Grilled Stuffed Artichokes*

*Gratin of Fennel*

*Glazed Onions*

*Rack of Lamb with Mustard Crust*

*Mint Chutney*

*George J.'s French Toast*

The mighty Mississippi is a highway of many great flavors traveling in and out of New Orleans. When the Spanish arrived in New Orleans in the late eighteenth century with their tomatoes and garlic, they threw the French already there into a dither. The situation was further complicated by the arrival of wealthy French, who were escaping the French Revolution. These historical incidents became the basis of Creole cuisine. Around the same time, some French peasants living in Acadia were driven out by the British and settled in the Louisiana bayous. Their name was mispronounced, and eventually they became known as Cajun. Some people describe the difference between Creole and Cajun cuisines as the contrast between city cooking and country cooking. This menu commemorates the freedom all people seek in our country.

# Grilled Stuffed Artichokes

### Makes 4 servings

*Grill temperature*

**medium**

**A**rtichokes are a double challenge: the first is preparing them for cooking and the second is eating them. They do look intimidating with that little spike at the tip of each leaf, but once the tips have been cut off, the rest is easy. For those who have never eaten an artichoke, you put the base end of the leaf in your mouth and scrape off the soft flesh with your teeth.

**4 large artichokes**
**Juice of 1 lemon**
**½ pound hot Italian sausage, grilled (page 305) and removed from casing**
**1 cup bread crumbs**
**½ cup olive oil**
**½ small onion, sliced, grilled (page 303), and chopped**
**¼ cup grated Parmesan cheese**
**Puree from 8 cloves Caramelized Garlic (page 302)**
**½ teaspoon dried basil**
**½ teaspoon dried oregano**
**Freshly ground black pepper**

*Gather 'Round the Grill*

**C**ut the stems from the artichokes and remove any tough outer leaves. Lay the artichokes on their sides on a flat surface and, using a sharp knife, cut off the top ½ inch. Using a kitchen shear, snip off ¼ inch from the tops of the leaves. Place the artichokes in a saucepan, add the lemon juice, and cover with water. Bring the water to a boil on the stovetop, lower the heat, and simmer 10 minutes. Drain the artichokes, reserving 1 cup of the cooking liquid. Place the artichokes upside down and let cool. Spread the leaves open, scrape out the choke with a teaspoon, and discard.

**P**reheat the grill.

**I**n a medium bowl combine the sausage, bread crumbs, ¼ cup of the olive oil, onion, cheese, garlic, basil, oregano, and black pepper and mix well. Fill the center cavities of the artichokes evenly with this mixture, stuffing any excess between the leaves. Brush the artichokes with some of the remaining olive oil and grill 2 to 3 minutes. Place them in an ovenproof pan with ½ cup of the cooking liquid and any remaining olive oil. Bake, uncovered, for 20 to 25 minutes, with the grill cover down, adding additional liquid if necessary.

# Gratin of Fennel

**Makes 4 servings**

*Grill temperature*

**medium, then low**

**R**aw fennel has a slight anise flavor, but once it's cooked, the flavor becomes light and delicate. It's also called finocchio and is available from fall through spring.

**1 recipe Grilled Fennel (page 252)**

**1 cup heavy cream**

**½ teaspoon Tabasco**

**¼ cup bread crumbs**

**¼ cup grated Parmesan cheese**

**P**reheat the grill.

**P**lace the cooked fennel in a buttered shallow casserole. Combine the cream and Tabasco and pour over the fennel. Top evenly with the bread crumbs and Parmesan cheese. Place on the upper shelf of hot grill, lower the lid, and cook until bubbly and slightly brown, about 10 minutes.

# Glazed Onions

### Makes 4 servings

The humble onion gets the royal treatment with this sweet and spicy glaze.

Grill
temperature

**medium**

**¼ cup (½ stick) butter or margarine**

**2 tablespoons light corn syrup**

**1 teaspoon ground thyme**

**½ teaspoon ground allspice**

**¼ teaspoon Tabasco**

**Pinch ground nutmeg**

**1½ cups pearl onions, cooked, or 1½ Spanish onions, grilled (page 303)**

Preheat the grill or side burner.

Melt the butter in a skillet on the grill or side burner and stir in the corn syrup, thyme, allspice, Tabasco, and nutmeg. Add the onions and cook, stirring occasionally, until they turn golden brown, about 5 to 7 minutes.

*Spring*
*Menu 6*

# Rack of Lamb with Mustard Crust

**Makes 2 servings**

*Grill temperature*

**high-medium**

**W**hen buying lamb, let color be your guide: the darker the flesh, the older the animal. Have your butcher remove the chine bone before grilling and carving will be a cinch. The flavor of mint always seems to complement lamb, and if you've always liked mint jelly with lamb, you'll love it with Mint Chutney.

> **1 rack of lamb**
> **Lamb Marinade (recipe follows)**
> **Puree from 4 cloves Caramelized Garlic (page 302)**
> **1 cup bread crumbs**
> **2 tablespoons Dijon mustard**
> **1 tablespoon grated Parmesan cheese**
> **1 tablespoon olive oil**
> **½ teaspoon Tabasco**
> **Mint Chutney (page 66)**

*Gather 'Round the Grill*

**M**arinate the rack of lamb in the marinade for 24 hours before grilling.

**P**reheat the grill.

**T**o make the mustard crust combine the garlic, bread crumbs, mustard, Parmesan cheese, olive oil, and Tabasco in a small bowl and mix well.

**P**lace the lamb on the grill, meat down, and grill for 10 minutes, watching carefully not to burn the meat if the fire should flare up. Remove the rack and pat the crust mixture on the meat side. Return the lamb to the grill, crust side up, and cook an additional 15 minutes for medium-rare. Remove the rack from the grill and let rest 15 minutes before slicing. Serve with chutney.

## Lamb Marinade

**Makes about ²/₃ cup**

½ cup olive oil

3 cloves garlic, sliced

1 teaspoon dried rosemary, crushed

1 teaspoon dried thyme

½ teaspoon coarse black pepper

1 tablespoon balsamic vinegar

**C**ombine all the ingredients in a small nonreactive bowl and mix well.

(*continued*)

*Spring
Menu 6*

# Mint Chutney

**Makes about 1 cup**

**M**ake this chutney a few hours in advance so that the flavors have a chance to meld.

> ¼ **cup chopped fresh mint**
>
> ¼ **cup chopped scallions**
>
> ¼ **cup plain yogurt**
>
> **1 tablespoon light corn syrup**
>
> **2 tablespoons chopped toasted walnuts (page 303)**
>
> **Juice and zest of 1 lemon**
>
> ½ **teaspoon Tabasco**

**P**lace all the ingredients in a blender or food processor and blend for 2 to 3 minutes.

# George J.'s French Toast

**Makes 4 servings**

I was ten years old when I was allowed to solo on the grill. I've prepared this recipe many a time for my father while we were fishing or camping out. He knew of my love of cooking with garlic, and always swore that my secret ingredient in this recipe was garlic. I know he's still telling stories of the French toast and the big fish that got away.

> **4 eggs, separated**
>
> **4 tablespoons sugar**
>
> **1 tablespoon orange juice**
>
> **1 teaspoon vanilla extract**
>
> **1 teaspoon ground cinnamon**
>
> **1 loaf day-old French bread, cut on the diagonal into 1-inch slices**
>
> **4 tablespoons (½ stick) margarine**
>
> **Confectioners' sugar, maple syrup, or stewed fruit**

**P**reheat the grill.

**I**n a medium bowl beat the egg yolks with 2 tablespoons of the sugar for 4 to 5 minutes or until light and creamy. Stir in the orange juice, vanilla, and cinnamon. In a second bowl beat the egg whites until soft peaks form, then beat in the remaining

*Spring
Menu 6*

**67**

2 tablespoons sugar. Gently fold the egg whites into the egg yolk mixture. Dip the slices of bread into the batter and place on hot, well-seasoned grill. Cook for 30 seconds, turn the slices over, and grill until light brown.

**M**elt 2 tablespoons of the margarine in a large skillet on the grill. As the French toast comes off the grill, place the pieces in the skillet and brown on both sides, adding the remaining margarine as needed. Sprinkle the French toast with confectioners' sugar or drizzle with maple syrup or serve with stewed fruit.

# Menu 7

*Chili Wings*

*Five-Alarm Chili*

*Chili Potatoes*

*Vegetable Chips with Beer Cheese Dip*

*Apple Crisp*

Firefighters take turns with the firehouse cooking chores, and they are great grillers. When they prepare a dish, it has to be one that can be interrupted during cooking in case there's a burning building that needs attention or a cat that needs rescuing. Some of their adventures in cooking are so successful that several firehouse cookbooks have been published. Let's take our hats off to the cooks who really know their fire.

# Chili Wings

**Makes 4 servings**

*Grill temperature*

**medium-high**

Chicken wings were once considered good enough only for the soup pot, but since the arrival of Buffalo chicken wings, we can't seem to find enough ways of preparing them. Here's a version that is sweet and hot rather than sweet and sour. Scotch bonnets are small peppers, but don't let their size fool you. They're one of the hottest peppers around.

**1 cup pineapple juice**

**2 tablespoons balsamic vinegar**

**2 tablespoons dark brown sugar**

**4 cloves garlic, minced**

**1 or 2 Scotch bonnet peppers or jalapeños, chopped**

**½ teaspoon ground allspice**

**Salt and pepper to taste**

**¼ cup ice**

**12 chicken wings**

To make the marinade, combine the pineapple juice, balsamic vinegar, brown sugar, garlic, peppers, allspice, salt, and pepper in a small saucepan, and boil 2 minutes. Add the ice and set aside until cool.

Cut the wings into 3 pieces each and discard the small wing tip (or save for soup). Place the chicken wings and the marinade in a bowl and refrigerate a minimum of 2 hours (or overnight).

Preheat the grill.

Remove the wings from the marinade and cook slowly on the grill for 15 to 20 minutes, turning occasionally.

# Five-Alarm Chili

**Makes 8 servings**

**I**n firehouse jargon, the higher the number of the alarm, the hotter the fire, so adjust the degree of hotness in this chili by raising or lowering the amount of chilies. Chili originated in Texas as a "bowl of red." Authentic recipes call for beef and shun the beans, but if you're not in Texas, you can do as you like.

½ cup **Pork Dry Rub (page 74)**

2 pounds **boneless beef round**

1 pound **boneless pork loin chops**

2 tablespoons **olive oil**

½ pound **smoked ham, grilled (page 305) and diced**

2 medium **onions, thickly sliced, grilled (page 303) and diced**

½ cup **chopped scallions**

**Puree from 1 head Caramelized Garlic (page 302)**

2 tablespoons **ground cumin**

1 tablespoon **ground coriander**

1 tablespoon **dried basil**

1 teaspoon **dried oregano**

2 tablespoons **ground chilies, such as ancho or serrano**

2 cups **grilled tomatoes (page 303), chopped**

2 cups **tomato puree**

**1 cup catsup**

**2 tablespoons cider vinegar**

**2 bay leaves**

**2 cups cooked kidney beans**

Rub the pork rub onto all sides of the beef and pork chops and refrigerate 2 hours.

Preheat the grill.

Place the beef and pork chops on the grill and sear over high heat for 2 to 3 minutes on each side. Cool slightly and cut into ½-inch cubes.

Heat the oil in a large stockpot on the grill over high heat. Add the ham, onions, scallions, garlic, cumin, coriander, basil, and oregano and cook until light brown. Add the chilies and stir well. Add the beef, pork, tomatoes, tomato puree, catsup, vinegar, and bay leaves. Stir well, lower the heat, and simmer 1½ hours or until the meat is cooked.

Add the beans to the pot and simmer 30 minutes longer. Remove the bay leaves.

(continued)

*Spring
Menu 7*

# Pork Dry Rub

**Makes about 1 cup**

¼ cup hot paprika

2 tablespoons dried thyme

2 tablespoons dried rosemary

2 tablespoons garlic powder

1 tablespoon ground cumin

1 tablespoon dried oregano

½ teaspoon ground black pepper

½ teaspoon ground nutmeg

¼ teaspoon cayenne

Combine all ingredients in a small bowl and mix well.

# Chili Potatoes

**Makes 4 servings**

I couldn't decide whether to cook these potatoes in a pot or on the grill, so I wound up doing both and the result is a terrific potato recipe.

*Grill temperature*

**high, then medium**

**12 medium new red potatoes**

**¼ cup olive oil**

**Puree from 8 cloves Caramelized Garlic (page 302)**

**1 teaspoon Tabasco**

**2 teaspoons ground cumin**

**2 teaspoons dried thyme**

**2 tablespoons margarine**

**2 teaspoons chopped fresh cilantro**

**Freshly ground black pepper**

On a stovetop, blanch the potatoes in boiling water for 5 minutes and drain well. In a medium bowl combine the olive oil, garlic, Tabasco, cumin, and thyme. Toss the potatoes lightly in this mixture and marinate for 30 minutes.

Preheat the grill.

Quickly sear the potatoes over high heat on the grill for 2 to 3 minutes. In a medium saucepan melt the margarine on the grill over medium heat, add the potatoes, and cook 2 minutes, tossing them in the pan occasionally. Drizzle the potatoes with any remaining marinade. Place in a serving bowl and top with cilantro and black pepper.

*Spring Menu 7*

**75**

# Vegetable Chips with Beer Cheese Dip

## Makes 4 servings

**M**ost root vegetables can be deep-fried and they're just as crisp and delicious as potato chips. Heat a kettle of oil to 360° F. on the grill or side burner and fry away.

Make sure you make enough of these chips to go around. They disappear quite readily. When Vegetable Chips was on the menu at my restaurant, we had to take it off because we couldn't prepare enough of them fast enough.

> **Vegetable oil, for frying**
> **1 russet potato, peeled and thinly sliced**
> **1 sweet potato, peeled and thinly sliced**
> **1 taro root, peeled and thinly sliced**
> **1 yucca, peeled and thinly sliced**
> **1 plantain, peeled and thinly sliced**
> **1 lotus root, peeled and thinly sliced**
> **Sea salt to taste**
> **Beer Cheese Dip (recipe follows)**

**P**reheat the grill.

Pour the vegetable oil in a deep kettle and heat to 360° F. Pat the vegetable slices dry and fry a few at a time in the hot oil until crisp. Drain on paper towels and sprinkle with sea salt.

Serve with Beer Cheese Dip.

# Beer Cheese Dip

### Makes 4 cups

Grill
temperature

**low**

You can change the character of this dip by substituting Grilled Salsa (page 143) for the beer or by adding 4 grilled jalapeño peppers or ½ package of defrosted chopped frozen spinach. Serve with grilled flour tortillas or vegetable chips.

> **2 cups shredded Monterey Jack cheese (8 ounces)**
>
> **2 cups shredded Cheddar cheese (8 ounces)**
>
> **8 ounces cream cheese, cut into pieces, at room temperature**
>
> **Puree from 1 head Caramelized Garlic (page 302)**
>
> **½ teaspoon dry mustard**
>
> **½ teaspoon Tabasco**
>
> **½ teaspoon Worcestershire sauce**
>
> **One 12-ounce bottle beer**

Preheat the grill or side burner.

In a medium saucepan combine the Monterey Jack, Cheddar, cream cheese, garlic, dry mustard, Tabasco, and Worcestershire sauce. Stirring constantly, heat the mixture over grill or on side burner. Slowly stir in the beer and mix well.

Spring
Menu 7

# Apple Crisp

**Makes 6 to 8 servings**

*Grill temperature*

**medium**

**A**ny variety of apple can be used to make a crisp, but the combination of Granny Smith and McIntosh apples lends lots of flavor. The granola gives the crisp topping some extra crunch.

**4 to 5 apples, peeled, cored, halved, and grilled (page 305)**

**½ cup light or dark brown sugar**

**½ cup (1 stick) margarine, softened**

**2 teaspoons ground cinnamon**

**¾ cup all-purpose flour**

**1 cup granola**

**1 cup sugar**

**Juice of 1 lemon**

**P**reheat the grill.

**C**ool the grilled apples slightly, then slice ½ inch thick.

**I**n a small bowl combine the brown sugar, margarine, and 1 teaspoon cinnamon; blend well. Add the flour and knead the mixture until it forms crumbs the size of shelled peanuts. Toss in the granola and mix lightly. Place half the crumb mixture on the bottom of a well-buttered 2-quart, ovenproof pan. In a separate bowl mix the remaining teaspoon of cinnamon and the granulated sugar. Sprinkle this mixture over the apples, and drizzle with the lemon juice. Top the apples with the remaining crumb-granola mixture. Place the pan on a raised shelf or construct a shelf with a few bricks. Bake the crisp with the grill lid down for 35 to 40 minutes. Serve warm or cold.

*Gather 'Round the Grill*

Summer

# Menu 8

*Smoked Duck*

*Crab Chowder*

*Swiss Chard and Pears*

*Split Leg of Lamb with Pepper and Lemon*

*Stuffed Peaches*

**W**hen the sun is shining and the weather's perfect, it's easy to be intimate with the outdoors. This is the kind of day to go to the market and buy some new food like Swiss chard that you have never cooked before. More and more cities are opening old-style farmer's markets, where you can buy vegetables directly from the people who planted and nurtured them. Create a meal to share with someone you really care for and arm-in-arm you can create your own new traditions.

# Smoked Duck

### Makes 4 servings

**S**ince it takes time to set up a smoker and even longer for the food to cook, it's a good idea to cook some extra food while the smoker is going. Even a small amount of smoked meats and vegetables add a lot of flavor to soups, appetizers, salads, or pastas.

Smoked fruit, such as apples or pears, or grilled fruit, such as pineapple or peaches, would taste wonderful with this duck.

> **1 cup Dry Poultry Rub (recipe follows)**
> **Two 4½-pound Long Island ducks, split in half**
> **1 cup apple cider**
> **1 cup light corn syrup**
> **¼ cup cider vinegar**

**H**eavily rub the dry rub onto all sides of the ducks 2 days prior to smoking. The coating should be ⅛ inch thick. Place the ducks in a shallow pan and refrigerate uncovered.

**E**ight hours before you heat the smoker, shake the excess rub off the ducks and return them to the shallow pan. Pour in the apple cider, corn syrup, and cider vinegar and refrigerate.

**P**repare a water smoker for 4 hours. Allow 1 hour for the charcoal to heat up before adding the food, preferably with applewood (or other fruitwood) that has been soaked for 1 hour.

Remove the ducks from the pan and place them on the grill. Pour the marinade into the smoker's water pan. Smoke the ducks for 3 to 4 hours or until the meat registers 195° F. on an instant-read thermometer.

## Dry Poultry Rub

**Makes about 1 1/8 cups**

1/4 cup sweet paprika

2 tablespoons brown sugar

1 tablespoon dried rosemary, crumbled

1 tablespoon dried parsley

1 tablespoon garlic powder

1 tablespoon chopped fresh sage

1/4 teaspoon ground nutmeg

Combine all ingredients in a small bowl and mix well.

# Crab Chowder

**Makes 6 to 8 servings**

*Grill temperature*

**medium, then low**

**M**any a feud has taken place as to whether a *real* chowder has a cream or a tomato base. If you have leanings toward the white kind, give this red-based one a try and decide for yourself.

2 tablespoons butter

1 medium onion, thickly sliced, grilled (page 303), and coarsely chopped

3 ribs celery, chopped

2 green bell peppers, grilled (page 302), seeded, and diced

Puree from 8 cloves Caramelized Garlic (page 302)

8 fresh mushrooms, grilled (page 303) and sliced

1 cup tomato puree

6 cups fish or chicken stock

1 cup chopped grilled (page 303) tomatoes

4 scallions, grilled (page 303) and chopped

1 pound lump crab meat

1 teaspoon dried thyme

1 teaspoon dried oregano

1 teaspoon dried parsley

½ teaspoon Tabasco

2 bay leaves

*Gather 'Round the Grill*

**P**reheat the grill or side burner.

**H**eat the butter in a 4-quart pot on the grill or side burner. Add the onion, celery, green peppers, garlic, and mushrooms and simmer 2 to 3 minutes. Add the tomato puree and cook 2 minutes. Add the stock and bring to a boil. Add the tomatoes, scallions, half the crab meat, the thyme, oregano, parsley, Tabasco, and bay leaves. Reduce heat and simmer 15 minutes. Add remaining crab meat and simmer 2 to 3 minutes. Discard bay leaves.

# Swiss Chard and Pears

**Makes 4 servings**

*Grill temperature*
**medium-high**

**S**wiss chard is one of those underutilized green vegetables, especially since it must be thoroughly washed. Although Swiss chard is considered a bitter vegetable, try it with pears and you may never go back to spinach again.

**1 bunch Swiss chard, stems removed
(use them in soup or cooked in a salad)**

**3 Bartlett pears, cored and sliced into thin slivers**

**2 tablespoons olive oil**

**1 tablespoon balsamic vinegar**

**1 tablespoon toasted walnuts (page 303)**

**Freshly ground black pepper to taste**

**P**reheat the grill.

**B**lanch the chard in boiling water on the stovetop for 2 minutes, then remove. Brush the pears with some of the olive oil and place on the grill, turning once after 2 minutes. Remove and place in a serving bowl. Brush the chard with the remaining oil and toss quickly directly on the grill. Remove the chard and combine with the pear slices. Add the balsamic vinegar and walnuts and toss gently. Sprinkle with black pepper.

*Summer Menu 8*

# Split Leg of Lamb with Pepper and Lemon

### Makes 8 servings

*Grill temperature*

**medium-low**

**M**any people think of lamb as a springtime meat, but it's abundant all seasons of the year and makes a great choice when inviting a crowd because it very easily feeds a lot of people.

If you like your lamb with a crispy crust, place the meat directly over the fire for the last ten minutes of cooking.

> **1 head garlic, cloves separated and peeled**
> **Juice and zest of 2 lemons**
> **2 tablespoons coarsely ground black pepper**
> **6- to 7-pound leg of lamb, boned and split**
> **Lamb Basting Sauce (recipe follows)**

**P**lace the garlic on a cutting board, cover with the side of a large chef's knife, press down lightly, and smash the cloves. Combine the garlic with the lemon juice, lemon zest, and black pepper. Rub this mixture onto both sides of the lamb and marinate for 24 hours in the refrigerator.

**P**reheat the grill.

*Gather 'Round the Grill*

**P**lace the marinated lamb on the grill with a disposable aluminum pan beneath the grate to catch the drippings. Baste the lamb with the basting sauce every 5 to 10 minutes. Cook approximately 30 minutes for medium-rare, 40 to 45 minutes for well done. Cover the lamb and allow to stand 15 to 20 minutes before slicing so the meat will reabsorb the juices.

# Lamb Basting Sauce

**Makes 1 ¹/₂ cups**

**1 cup honey**

**¹/₄ cup balsamic vinegar**

**¹/₄ cup chopped fresh mint**

**1 teaspoon sea salt**

In a small bowl combine all the ingredients and mix well.

*Summer*
*Menu 8*

# Stuffed Peaches

### Makes 4 servings

*Grill temperature*

**medium-low**

**A**t my restaurant in Kings Park, New York, we had a customer named Brian who had a rather large sweet tooth and always looked forward to dessert. We were constantly on the lookout for new and different ways to please Brian. One day, near the end of peach season, we came up with this one. Brian was very happy.

- **8 tablespoons (1 stick) butter**
- **2 tablespoons granulated sugar**
- **2 tablespoons brown sugar**
- **4 tablespoons finely chopped walnuts**
- **2 tablespoons dried cookie crumbs**
- **1 tablespoon all-purpose flour**
- **1 teaspoon ground cinnamon**
- **4 large peaches, cut in half and pitted**

**P**reheat the grill.

**I**n a small bowl combine 4 tablespoons of butter and both sugars and mix well. Add the walnuts, cookie crumbs, flour, and cinnamon. Fill 4 peach halves evenly with the mixture. Top with the remaining halves. Melt the remaining 4 tablespoons butter and brush the peaches, place them on the grill, and cook, turning once, until the filling begins to melt.

# Menu 9

*Louie's Stuffed Calamari*

*Basil Dressing*

*Grilled Chicken with Watercress*

*Mustard New Potatoes*

*Grouper with Orange on a Bed of Fresh Spinach*

*Chocolate Cream Pie*

Some men and women rejoice at the thought of retiring. Others dread the gold watch even when it's accompanied by a golden parachute. Still others look forward to retirement as the time to clean out the tackle box or start taking piano lessons. This menu will help you celebrate retiring from work as well as appreciate that extra time there'll be to gather 'round the grill.

# Louie's Stuffed Calamari

## Makes 4 servings

**C**alamari, or squid, is one of those sea creatures you either love passionately or refuse to have pass your lips. When stuffed, it can be served with your favorite tomato sauce or the Basil Dressing. You can change the flavor of the stuffing by substituting chopped shrimp in place of the clams or by adding some smoky ham for extra flavor.

> **12 large squid**
>
> **½ cup chopped fresh or canned clams, with juice**
>
> **1 egg, lightly beaten**
>
> **2 tablespoons bread crumbs**
>
> **1 tablespoon dried parsley**
>
> **1 tablespoon grated Parmesan cheese**
>
> **Puree from 2 cloves Caramelized Garlic (page 302)**
>
> **2 tablespoons olive oil**
>
> **Basil Dressing (recipe follows)**

**P**reheat the grill.

**C**lean the squid and remove the tentacles. Leave the bodies whole and chop the tentacles. In a medium bowl mix the chopped tentacles, clams, egg, bread crumbs, parsley, Parmesan cheese, and garlic. Stuff the squid cavities evenly with the mixture and brush with the olive oil. Do not overstuff. Place the squid on the grill and cook until the flesh turns white, 2 to 3 minutes on each side. Be careful they don't overcook.

# Basil Dressing

**Makes almost ¾ cup**

¼ cup olive oil

¼ cup chopped fresh basil

Juice of 1 lemon

Puree from 3 cloves Caramelized Garlic (page 302)

½ teaspoon freshly ground black pepper

¼ teaspoon Tabasco

Pinch sea salt

Combine all the ingredients in a bowl and mix well. Heat the dressing slightly and pour over stuffed calamari just before serving.

*Summer
Menu 9*

# Grilled Chicken with Watercress

**Makes 4 servings**

**W**atercress has a peppery taste that holds up well to highly seasoned foods. If you can't find it, substitute arugula.

> **2 tablespoons olive oil**
>
> **1 tablespoon balsamic vinegar**
>
> **1 teaspoon chopped fresh cilantro**
>
> **Pinch ground allspice**
>
> **4 large boneless and skinless chicken breast halves**
>
> **2 bunches watercress, cleaned, stems removed**
>
> **1 cup croutons**
>
> **2 tablespoons grated Parmesan cheese**
>
> **Freshly ground black pepper**
>
> **½ cup Grilled Chicken Vinaigrette (recipe follows)**

**I**n a shallow bowl combine the olive oil, balsamic vinegar, cilantro, and allspice. Add the chicken breasts and marinate for 1 hour.

**P**reheat the grill.

**P**lace the chicken on the grill and cook 3 to 4 minutes. Turn the pieces over and cook until chicken is done, 3 to 4 minutes longer.

**W**ash the watercress, pat dry, and arrange on 4 plates. Slice the chicken breasts and arrange on the watercress. Scatter the croutons on top, then sprinkle with the Parmesan cheese and black pepper. Drizzle 2 tablespoons of the vinaigrette over each serving.

# Grilled Chicken Vinaigrette

**Makes about 1 cup**

**Juice of 1 lemon**

**2 tablespoons grated Parmesan cheese**

**1 tablespoon cider vinegar**

**1 tablespoon Dijon mustard**

**1 tablespoon anchovy puree**

**Puree from 6 cloves Caramelized Garlic (page 302)**

**⅔ cup olive oil**

In a small bowl whisk together the lemon juice, cheese, vinegar, mustard, anchovy puree, and garlic. Slowly beat in the olive oil, then let flavors blend for about 2 hours. Mix well and serve.

Summer
Menu 9

# Mustard New Potatoes

**Makes 4 to 6 servings**

*Grill temperature*

**medium-low**

Some like them hot and some like them cold, but one can never have too many recipes for potato salad. This one has a mustard dressing that gets a little extra zip from capers.

**1 to 1½ pounds baby new red potatoes**

**1 medium onion, sliced ¼ inch thick, grilled (page 303), and chopped**

**2 tablespoons Dijon mustard**

**Puree from 4 cloves Caramelized Garlic (page 302)**

**1 tablespoon capers, rinsed**

**1 teaspoon chopped fresh parsley**

**1 teaspoon chopped fresh chives**

**1 teaspoon chopped fresh mint**

**½ teaspoon Tabasco**

**4 tablespoons olive oil**

**Juice of 2 lemons**

On the stovetop, cook the potatoes in lightly salted water until tender, 18 to 20 minutes. Cut the potatoes into 1-inch pieces.

*Gather 'Round the Grill*

In a medium bowl combine the potato and onion. In a separate bowl combine the mustard, garlic, capers, parsley, chives, mint, and Tabasco. Stir in the olive oil and the lemon juice and mix well. Toss with the potatoes and marinate 1 hour before serving.

# Grouper with Orange on a Bed of Fresh Spinach

**Makes 4 servings**

To improve its flavor, make the marinade several hours in advance and let it sit at room temperature before adding the grouper. This marinade is very versatile, so if grouper isn't available, substitute monkfish, mahimahi, swordfish, salmon, or shark.

*Grill temperature*

**high**

½ **cup orange juice**

¼ **cup olive oil**

1 **tablespoon balsamic vinegar**

1 **teaspoon orange zest**

½ **teaspoon ground thyme**

¼ **teaspoon coarsely ground black pepper**

¼ **teaspoon Tabasco**

2 **pounds grouper fillets**

8 **scallions, trimmed**

8 **mushroom caps, either button or shiitake**

4 **cups fresh spinach, washed and well drained**

In a small bowl combine the orange juice, olive oil, balsamic vinegar, orange zest, thyme, black pepper, and Tabasco and mix well.

*(continued)*

*Summer Menu 9*

**P**lace the marinade in an ovenproof baking dish with the fish, scallions, and mushroom caps and marinate for 15 minutes.

**P**reheat the grill.

**G**rill the fish for 3 minutes. Turn the fish and cook 2 minutes. When the fish is cooked, return it to the baking dish. Grill the scallions and mushrooms until the mushrooms are tender, about 3 to 5 minutes.

**A**rrange the scallions and mushrooms around the grouper. Place the pan on the grill and heat until the sauce begins to boil, about 2 minutes. Line a serving platter with the spinach and arrange the fish, scallions, and mushroom caps on top. Pour the cooking juices over the fish.

# Chocolate Cream Pie

**Makes 6 to 8 servings**

*Grill temperature*

**medium**

I begin this menu with Louie's recipe for Stuffed Calamari. Louie is my father-in-law and his favorite dessert is chocolate cream pie. So I'm capping off the menu in his honor with his number one pie.

> ¾ cup sugar
>
> 2 tablespoons cornstarch
>
> 3 eggs, lightly beaten
>
> 1 teaspoon vanilla extract
>
> 2 cups milk
>
> 2 tablespoons (1 ounce) finely chopped semisweet chocolate
>
> 1 tablespoon butter
>
> 1 prebaked 9-inch pie shell
>
> Whipped cream, for garnish

Preheat the grill.

In a medium bowl combine the sugar and cornstarch and mix well. Stir in the eggs and vanilla. In a saucepan on the grill, heat the milk, chocolate, and butter until the mixture comes to a boil. Add 1 cup of the chocolate mixture to the cornstarch mixture and stir well. Return to the saucepan and, gently stirring, slowly bring the mixture to a boil. Remove from heat and pour into the prebaked pie shell. Cool 20 to 30 minutes and refrigerate 4 hours. Serve with whipped cream.

*Summer Menu 9*

**97**

# Menu 10

*Pasta with Mussels in a Green Sauce*

*Onion and Honey Salad*

*Chili-Rub Flank Steak with Corn Salsa*

*Toasted Pineapple with Rum and Coconut*

Will Rogers once called San Antonio one of the four unique cities in the United States (the others being Boston, San Francisco, and New Orleans). Part Spanish and part Mexican, San Antonio is set among palm trees and banana plants. Although it has evolved into a modern city, it still retains much of the flavor of its past. There's the Mission Trail, the museums, the breweries, Market Square, the zoo, and of course, the Alamo, smack in the middle of downtown. Remember the Alamo, the "Cradle of Texas Liberty," and celebrate this symbol of American frontier spirit.

# Pasta with Mussels in a Green Sauce

## Makes 4 servings

*Grill temperature*

**medium-high, then medium**

**I**f the mere thought of cream and butter raises your cholesterol, substitute chicken stock for the butter and white wine for the cream.

**1 pound linguine**

**6 tablespoons olive oil**

**3 pounds mussels, preferably farm-raised, washed and debearded**

**1 cup dry white wine**

**Puree from 1 head Caramelized Garlic (page 302)**

**2 cups Green Sauce (recipe follows)**

**2 tablespoons butter**

**½ cup heavy cream**

**C**ook the linguine until al dente. Drain well, place in a serving bowl, and toss with 2 tablespoons of the olive oil. Keep pasta warm while preparing the sauce.

**P**reheat the grill.

**H**eat remaining 4 tablespoons olive oil in a large stockpot on grill, then add the mussels, wine, and garlic. Cover the pot tightly and cook for 5 to 7 minutes or until the mussels open. Discard any mussels that do not open.

*Gather 'Round the Grill*

**100**

Remove the mussels from the pot, add the sauce and butter to the juices in the pot, and simmer over medium heat 3 to 4 minutes.

Remove the meat from the mussel shells and add to the pot along with the cream. Bring to a boil and toss with the cooked linguine.

# Green Sauce

### Makes about 2 cups

8 to 10 chili peppers, such as poblano, Anaheim, or jalapeño

1 medium onion, thickly sliced

2 medium tomatillos or tomatoes, quartered

½ cup chopped fresh cilantro

¼ cup chopped fresh Italian parsley

2 tablespoons olive oil

Juice of 1 lime

Grill
temperature

high

Preheat the grill.

Grill the chili peppers, quickly charring them on the outside so their skins begin to peel. Grill the onion and the tomatillos. Cool all the vegetables. Remove the skins from the chilies. Puree the chilies, onion, tomatillos, cilantro, and parsley for 30 seconds in a blender or food processor. Add the olive oil and lime juice and blend 1 additional minute.

# Onion and Honey Salad

**Makes 4 servings**

**F**ew people are aware that there are many different types of onions. Experiment with some of the varieties you might find at various times of the year, such as Texas onions, Vidalia onions, Bermuda onions, or Maui onions. Sometimes the onions themselves are sweeter than the honey that goes into the salad.

**3 to 4 large red onions, sliced ½ inch thick**

**4 tablespoons olive oil**

**4 cups salad greens**

**2 red bell peppers, split, seeded, and grilled (page 302)**

**Juice of 2 lemons**

**2 tablespoons honey**

**2 tablespoons chopped fresh mint**

**Freshly ground black pepper**

**4 jalapeño peppers, grilled whole (page 303)**

**P**reheat the grill.

**B**rush the onion slices with 2 tablespoons of the olive oil and grill on both sides until slightly charred. Remove and arrange on the salad greens with the roasted red peppers.

**I**n a small bowl combine the remaining 2 tablespoons olive oil, lemon juice, honey, mint, and black pepper and mix well. Pour the dressing over the onions and top with the roasted jalapeños.

# Chili-Rub Flank Steak with Corn Salsa

**Makes 4 servings**

Grill
*temperature*
**high**

There was a time when flank steak was very inexpensive and there wasn't a great demand for it. But then it was put on the grill, its popularity soared, and its price rose.

If the price of flank steak is over your budget, you can use a top round London broil, but marinate it a little longer.

**2 teaspoons chili powder**

**2 teaspoons sweet paprika**

**2 teaspoons Tabasco**

**1 teaspoon freshly ground black pepper**

**1 teaspoon dried thyme**

**1 teaspoon dried oregano**

**1 teaspoon dried parsley**

**One 2-pound flank steak**

**¼ cup balsamic vinegar**

**¼ cup olive oil**

**¼ cup dry red wine**

**Juice of 1 lemon**

**Puree from 8 cloves Caramelized Garlic (page 302)**

**Corn Salsa (recipe follows)**

*Summer
Menu 10*

*(continued)*

In a small bowl combine the chili powder, paprika, Tabasco, black pepper, thyme, oregano, and parsley. Rub the mixture onto all sides of the flank steak and refrigerate 24 hours.

Remove the flank steak from the refrigerator. Combine the balsamic vinegar, olive oil, red wine, lemon juice, and garlic in a shallow bowl. Add the flank steak and refrigerate for an additional 24 hours.

Preheat the grill.

Grill the meat for 3 to 4 minutes, turn, and grill on second side for 3 to 4 minutes. Remove from the grill and let meat rest for 5 minutes before slicing across the grain. Serve with Corn Salsa.

## Corn Salsa

### Makes about 4 cups

2 cups plum tomatoes, grilled (page 303) and chopped

Kernels from 2 grilled ears of corn (page 303), or 1 (12-ounce) can corn kernels, drained

6 jalapeño peppers, grilled (page 303), seeded, and chopped

¼ cup chopped scallions

Puree from 6 cloves Caramelized Garlic (page 302)

Juice of 1 lime

1 tablespoon chopped fresh cilantro

In a medium bowl combine all the ingredients and mix well. Prepare the salsa at least 1 hour before serving.

# Toasted Pineapple with Rum and Coconut

### Makes 4 servings

**W**hen the warm weather approaches and you start thinking of Margaritas, daiquiris, and piña coladas, make this dessert. I'll bet you'll start hearing steel drums in the background.

> 1 ripe pineapple
> 1 cup light corn syrup
> ½ cup light or dark brown sugar
> ¼ cup rum
> 1 tablespoon orange juice
> 1 cup shredded coconut, toasted

**P**eel the pineapple, remove the core, and cut into finger-shape pieces.

**P**reheat the grill.

**I**n a small saucepan on a stovetop over high heat, combine the corn syrup, brown sugar, rum, and orange juice. Bring to a boil, lower heat, and simmer 2 to 3 minutes. Cool slightly.

**T**hread the pineapple fingers onto skewers and grill for 2 minutes. Turn and cook an additional 1 to 2 minutes, or until light brown. While the pineapple is still hot, dip it into the sugar syrup. Lift up the skewers so the excess drips off and then dip the pineapple into the coconut.

# Menu 11

Onion Bisque

Garlicky Lamb Riblets

Grilled Shrimp Salad

Seafood Sauce

Grilled Orange Pork Chops with Cranberry Dressing

Apple Charlotte

There's a lot going on in San Antonio. Each month some organization or other is holding a fiesta or a celebration like the Texas-Irish Festival on St. Patrick's Day, when they dye the river green, or the annual ten-day Fiesta San Antonio in April, when the whole town kicks up its heels. Even the Mission of San José has a mariachi mass every Sunday. In 1988, the U.S. Conference of Mayors voted San Antonio the most livable city in America. So get on the band wagon. No one wants to spend a lot of time cooking when there's a party going on in town. You deserve a day of celebration: a four-star menu without a four-star effort. Get the whole gang involved—kids, relatives, friends. Cheers! It's party time.

# Onion Bisque

**Makes 6 to 8 servings**

*Grill temperature*

**medium for vegetables; high, then low, for soup**

**I**f you don't live near an area where lobsters are plentiful or if they're out of season, make this soup and no one at the table will even ask where the lobsters are. It's sort of a lobster-onion bisque without the lobster. But a cup or two of cooked lobster meat added at the end can only make it better.

**2 tablespoons butter**

**3 large onions, sliced, grilled (page 303), and chopped**

**2 leeks, white part only, grilled (page 53) and chopped**

**Puree from 1 head Caramelized Garlic (page 302)**

**1 cup diced celery**

**2 tablespoons all-purpose flour**

**6 cups chicken stock**

**1 large potato, peeled and diced**

**2 to 3 plum tomatoes, grilled (page 303) and chopped**

**¼ cup tomato puree**

**2 bay leaves**

**1 teaspoon dried thyme leaves**

**½ teaspoon Tabasco**

**1 cup heavy cream**

**¼ cup dry sherry**

*Gather 'Round the Grill*

**P**reheat the grill and/or side burner.

**H**eat the butter in a 4-quart pot on the grill or side burner and add the onions, leeks, garlic, and celery. Cook 2 to 3 minutes or until the vegetables are golden brown.

Add the flour and cook 2 minutes, stirring constantly. Stir in the chicken stock, potato, plum tomatoes, tomato puree, bay leaves, thyme, and Tabasco. Bring the soup to a boil, lower heat or move to the cooler edge of the grill, and simmer for 20 to 25 minutes, or until the potato is tender. Stir in the cream and sherry and reheat, but do not boil. Discard bay leaves.

# Garlicky Lamb Riblets

**Makes 4 to 6 servings**

Y ou probably won't find lamb riblets at your supermarket. You'll have to order them from your butcher and he'll prepare them by trimming racks of lamb. Or for a more economical version, ask your butcher to cut up lamb breast.

*Grill temperature*
**medium-high**

½ **cup chopped fresh mint**
¼ **cup olive oil**
**Puree from 2 heads Caramelized Garlic (page 302)**
**Juice of 3 lemons**
¼ **teaspoon Tabasco**
**4 pounds lamb riblets**

Combine the mint, olive oil, garlic, lemon, and Tabasco in a shallow dish and marinate the lamb riblets in this mixture in the refrigerator for 24 hours.

Preheat the grill.

Place a pan beneath the grate to catch any drips and slowly grill the riblets for 8 to 10 minutes on each side, basting occasionally with the marinade. When the ribs are just about cooked, move them directly over the heat to crisp the outside, taking care not to burn them.

*Summer Menu 11*

# Grilled Shrimp Salad

**Makes 4 servings**

**M**any people like to start celebrating a special occasion with a cold shrimp cocktail. This version is more flavorful because the shrimp are marinated and then grilled. If you're a shrimp cocktail person, you'll recognize the sauce.

> **1 pound large shrimp, peeled and deveined**
>
> **1 cup Grilling Vinaigrette (recipe follows)**
>
> **4 large lettuce leaves**
>
> **2 ripe medium tomatoes, quartered**
>
> **2 hard-cooked eggs, quartered**
>
> **4 red onion slices, grilled (page 303)**
>
> **1 lemon, cut into wedges**
>
> **1 cup Seafood Sauce (page 112)**

**M**arinate the shrimp in the vinaigrette for 1 hour.

**P**reheat the grill.

**G**rill the shrimp over high heat for 2 minutes, lower heat to medium, and cook until done, about 4 to 5 minutes. Remove and chill.

**T**o serve, arrange the lettuce leaves on 4 plates and cover equally with the tomatoes, eggs, onion slices, and lemon. Serve with the Seafood Sauce on the side.

*Gather 'Round the Grill*

# Grilling Vinaigrette

**Makes about 1 cup**

¾ cup olive oil

1 tablespoon Dijon mustard

1 teaspoon dried parsley

1 teaspoon dried basil

1 teaspoon dried thyme

Puree from 2 cloves Caramelized Garlic (page 302)

¼ teaspoon Tabasco

Salt and pepper to taste

Juice of ½ lemon

1 tablespoon balsamic vinegar

1 tablespoon dry white wine

In a small bowl combine the olive oil, mustard, parsley, basil, thyme, garlic, Tabasco, salt, and pepper and whisk until well blended. Drizzle in the lemon juice, vinegar, and wine and mix well. Allow the vinaigrette to sit at room temperature for a day to improve its flavor.

*(continued)*

*Summer
Menu 11*

# Seafood Sauce

### Makes about 1 cup

This sauce has dual roles: a sauce for seafood and a dressing for grilled vegetables.

> ¾ cup mayonnaise
>
> 2 tablespoons catsup
>
> 2 tablespoons chili sauce
>
> Juice and zest of 1 lemon
>
> 1 tablespoon well-drained horseradish
>
> ½ teaspoon Tabasco
>
> ¼ teaspoon Worcestershire sauce

Combine all the ingredients in a small bowl, mix well, and refrigerate 2 hours.

# Grilled Orange Pork Chops with Cranberry Dressing

### Makes 4 servings

**W**hen most people serve fruit with pork chops, it's usually applesauce. And if they're serving cranberry sauce, it's most often with turkey. Here we've taken two good ideas and put them together. The cranberry sauce has a little vinegar in it, which makes it sweet-and-sour, not cloyingly sweet.

> **Juice and zest of 2 navel oranges**
>
> **2 tablespoons olive oil**
>
> **1 tablespoon chopped fresh cilantro**
>
> **Puree from 4 cloves Caramelized Garlic (page 302)**
>
> **1 teaspoon Tabasco**
>
> **½ teaspoon ground allspice**
>
> **Pinch ground nutmeg**
>
> **Four 7- to 8-ounce center-cut pork chops, about 1 inch thick**
>
> **Cranberry Dressing (recipe follows)**

**C**ombine the orange juice and zest, olive oil, cilantro, garlic, Tabasco, allspice, and nutmeg in a shallow bowl and mix well. Marinate the pork chops in this mixture for 1 hour in the refrigerator.

**P**reheat the grill.

**G**rill the pork chops for 7 to 8 minutes, turn, and cook another 7 to 8 minutes, or until done. Serve with the dressing.

*(continued)*

# Cranberry Dressing

**Makes about 2 ½ cups**

**2 cups fresh cranberries**
**¼ cup sugar**
**Juice of 1 orange**
**2 tablespoons cider vinegar**
**1 bay leaf**
**Freshly ground black pepper**

**B**ring all the ingredients to a boil in a medium saucepan. Lower heat, cover, and simmer 8 to 10 minutes. Remove bay leaf and serve.

# Apple Charlotte

**Makes 6 servings**

*Grill temperature*

**medium**

**N**ever throw out leftover bread or stale cookies because here's a perfect way to use them up. Raisin bread or cinnamon bread makes the charlotte even better tasting and gingersnaps or vanilla wafers are a welcome addition. If you don't have apples, use pears or firm peaches.

½ loaf day-old French bread, sliced very thin on an angle

4 cups sliced baking apples, such as Golden Delicious or Rome, grilled (page 305)

1 cup orange juice

½ cup raisins

4 tablespoons melted butter or margarine

1 cup crumbs from day-old cookies

¼ cup brown sugar

¼ cup granulated sugar

½ teaspoon ground cinnamon

Pinch ground nutmeg

Preheat the grill.

Butter an ovenproof baking dish and line with the French bread slices, then top evenly with the apple slices. Heat the orange juice with the raisins and pour over the apple slices. Pour 2 tablespoons of the melted butter over the apples.

In a small bowl combine the cookie crumbs, sugars, cinnamon, and nutmeg and mix well. Sprinkle this topping over the apples and drizzle with the remaining 2 tablespoons melted butter. Place on a raised rack in the grill and bake for 20 to 25 minutes with the grill cover down.

*Summer
Menu 11*

# Menu 12

*Sonoran Cheese Soup*

*Jalapeño Pizza*

*Triple Beans Refried*

*Mole Poblano*

*Pickled Watermelon*

Southwestern food is a conglomeration of flavors from the southern and western states of this country, influenced by the Mexican and Spanish cooks who have lived there. The tastes are bright and full, sometimes exploding in your mouth. These unique dishes were "invented" along the border towns where resourceful cooks made good use of whatever was in season. Tomatoes, beans, chilies, sweet peppers—all American foods indigenous to the New World. Invite relatives you haven't seen or heard from to a family reunion and start a new summer tradition.

# Sonoran Cheese Soup

### Makes 6 to 8 servings

*Grill temperature*

**medium, then low**

**M**ake this a day or two ahead so that the flavors get a chance to meld, but don't add the cheese until just before you are ready to serve.

2 tablespoons butter

1 large onion, thickly sliced, grilled (page 303), and chopped

1 large green bell pepper, grilled (page 302), seeded, and diced

6 to 8 green chili peppers

Puree from 1 head Caramelized Garlic (page 302)

2 tablespoons all-purpose flour

6 cups chicken stock

2 large potatoes, peeled and diced

1 cup corn kernels, from grilled corn on the cob (page 303) or canned corn

1 teaspoon chopped fresh cilantro

1 bay leaf

½ teaspoon ground cumin

½ teaspoon Tabasco

2 cups half-and-half

1 cup shredded Monterey Jack cheese

1 cup shredded Cheddar cheese

Grilled flour tortillas

*Gather 'Round the Grill*

**P**reheat the grill and side burner.

Heat the butter in a 4-quart pot on the side burner or grill. Add the onion, bell pepper, chili peppers, and garlic and cook 2 to 3 minutes. Stir in the flour and cook 2 minutes, stirring constantly. Add the stock, potatoes, corn, cilantro, bay leaf, cumin, and Tabasco. Bring to a boil, lower heat, and simmer 20 to 25 minutes. Add the half-and-half and bring to a simmer. Discard bay leaf. Stir in the cheeses until they just melt. Grill the tortillas over low heat and serve with soup.

# Jalapeño Pizza

**Makes 4 servings**

ne way to cut down on the hotness of the jalapeño peppers is to remove the seeds. You can make your own pizza dough or buy fresh or frozen dough in your supermarket or Italian market.

> ⅓ **cup sour cream**
>
> ⅓ **cup cream cheese, at room temperature**
>
> ⅓ **cup heavy cream**
>
> ¼ **cup roasted and chopped green bell pepper**
>
> **2 tablespoons chopped fresh cilantro**
>
> **Puree from 4 cloves Caramelized Garlic (page 302)**
>
> **2 pizza discs (page 304)**
>
> **Olive oil**
>
> **1 to 100 jalapeño peppers, grilled (page 303), split, and seeded**

**P**reheat the grill.

**P**uree the sour cream, cream cheese, heavy cream, green pepper, cilantro, and garlic in a blender or food processor. Divide the pizza dough in half, and on a lightly floured surface, roll each out into a 6-inch disc. Brush the pizza dough with olive oil and grill on one side. Remove, turn, brush with oil, and spread liberally with the topping to within ½ inch from the edge. Arrange as many jalapeños on top as it takes to reach your heat point. Place the pizza back on the grill and grill until the topping is warm and the crust is crisp, 2 to 4 minutes.

# Triple Beans Refried

**Makes 4 to 6 servings**

Grill temperature
**medium-low**

Turn this dish into a vegetarian entree by omitting the meat and topping the beans with Swiss or Monterey Jack cheese. Change it into a hearty main course by adding grilled chorizo or andouille sausage. The refried beans make a good filling for quesadillas or omelets.

> 4 slices bacon
> ½ cup grilled (page 303) and chopped onion
> Puree from 6 cloves Caramelized Garlic (page 302)
> 2 serrano peppers, grilled (page 303), seeded, and chopped
> 1½ cups cooked pinto beans
> 1½ cups cooked white beans
> 1½ cups cooked black beans
> ½ cup grilled (page 303) and chopped plum tomatoes
> 1 to 2 cups chicken or vegetable stock
> 1 teaspoon chopped fresh cilantro

Preheat the grill.

Cook the bacon in a large, heavy sauté pan on the grill, drain the bacon, chop and set aside. Add the onion, garlic, peppers, and beans to the bacon drippings in the pan and mix well. Stir in the tomatoes and 1 cup of the stock. Cook the beans 30 minutes, scraping the bottom of the pan occasionally so that the beans do not burn and adding the remaining stock as needed. The beans will slowly turn to mush. Top with the chopped bacon and cilantro.

Summer
Menu 12

# Mole Poblano

**Makes 4 servings**

**I**f you've never made mole poblano before, you might question that one of the ingredients is chocolate. The addition of a small amount of semisweet chocolate adds another level of flavor to the sauce. This recipe has a lot of ingredients and may seem a but complicated, but if you try it once you may hesitate the next time you want to run out for a bucket of chicken.

> **Four 8-ounce skinless and boneless chicken breasts**
> **2 tablespoons olive oil**
> **1 cup Mole Spice Mixture (recipe follows)**
> **1 cup chicken stock**
> **3 mulato, ancho, pasilla, or chipotle chili peppers**
> **(or a mixture of them), toasted and ground**
> **2 tablespoons margarine**
> **1 ounce semisweet chocolate, broken into small pieces**

**P**reheat the grill.

**B**rush the chicken breasts with olive oil and place on the grill over medium-low heat for 2 minutes on each side. They will not be fully cooked.

**P**lace the chicken breasts in a shallow pan with the spice mixture, stock, peppers, and margarine. Bring the mixture to a boil, lower the heat, and simmer 5 minutes. Add the chocolate and simmer until chocolate is melted and completely incorporated, 2 to 3 minutes longer.

# Mole Spice Mixture

**Makes about 2 cups**

4 tablespoons toasted (page 303) sesame seeds

2 tablespoons toasted (page 303) pumpkin seeds

¼ teaspoon anise seeds

½ teaspoon coriander seeds

¼ teaspoon cumin seeds

½ cup chopped grilled (page 303) plum tomatoes

½ cup chopped grilled (page 303) tomatillos

¼ fresh banana, peeled

1 flour tortilla, cut into small pieces

2 tablespoons raisins

2 tablespoons roasted peanuts

1 clove garlic

¼ teaspoon freshly ground black pepper

Pinch ground cinnamon

**P**lace all the seeds in a food grinder or blender and process until ground. Add the tomatoes, tomatillos, banana, tortilla, raisins, peanuts, garlic, and black pepper and process 2 to 3 minutes or until well blended.

# Pickled Watermelon

**Makes 12 servings**

**I**t seems that every successful barbecue or picnic is capped off with a slice of watermelon. This one will put a little surprise into everybody's dish.

> **1 medium watermelon**
> **One 6-ounce can frozen lemonade**
> **¼ cup finely chopped fresh mint**

**L**ay the watermelon on its side and cut out a 3-inch triangle. Defrost the lemonade and mix well with half the recommended amount of water and the mint. Pour this mixture into the watermelon, replace the plug, and chill 6 hours before serving.

# Menu 13

*Arugula Bruschetta*

*Pappardelle of Zucchini*

*Calzone*

*Pork Tenderloin with Garlic and Red Pepper Pesto*

*Plum Tart*

Food trends are said to begin on the East and West coasts and travel back and forth. Although I prepared this recipe on the East Coast, sometimes known for its wide range of cuisines, celebrate *your* food trends right in your own backyard and show off with a spin on the grill.

# Arugula Bruschetta

**Makes 4 servings**

**B**ruschetta are slices of toasted Tuscan bread brushed with olive oil and topped with chopped tomatoes and basil. These go a step further and include peppery arugula.

> **4 large slices Tuscan bread, ½ inch thick**
> **4 tablespoons olive oil**
> **1 cup roughly chopped arugula leaves**
> **2 plum tomatoes, split, grilled (page 303), and chopped**
> **Juice of 1 lemon**
> **Puree from 4 cloves Caramelized Garlic (page 302)**
> **4 basil leaves, chopped**

**P**reheat the grill.

**B**rush the bread with 2 tablespoons of the olive oil. In a small bowl combine the arugula, tomatoes, remaining 2 tablespoons olive oil, lemon juice, garlic, and basil. Grill the bread on both sides and top with the arugula mixture. Serve immediately.

# Pappardelle of Zucchini

**Makes 4 servings**

While hen the zucchini are cut in the shape of pappardelle, the finished dish looks more like pasta than vegetables.

*Grill temperature*

**high, then medium**

**2 medium or 3 small zucchini, sliced lengthwise into ribbons ⅛ inch wide**

**4 tablespoons olive oil**

**Puree from 6 cloves Caramelized Garlic (page 302)**

**1½ cups heavy cream**

**4 tablespoons grated Parmesan cheese**

**8 fresh basil leaves, chopped**

**½ teaspoon Tabasco**

**4 slices bacon, cooked and coarsely chopped**

**Freshly ground black pepper to taste**

Preheat the grill.

Brush the ribbons of zucchini with 2 tablespoons of the olive oil and grill over high heat for 2 to 3 minutes on each side.

In a separate saucepan, on grill or stovetop, heat the remaining 2 tablespoons olive oil, add the garlic, and cook 30 seconds over medium heat. Add the grilled zucchini and toss lightly. Stir in the cream, 2 tablespoons of Parmesan cheese, basil, and Tabasco and mix well. Transfer to a serving dish and top the zucchini with the bacon, remaining 2 tablespoons Parmesan cheese, and black pepper.

*Summer
Menu 13*

**127**

# Calzone

**Makes 4 servings**

**C**alzone comes from an Italian word that means "trouser leg" (the plural is *calzoni*), but it looks more like a turnover. Calzone is made from pizza dough and stuffed with many of the toppings you would use on a pizza. As one story goes, peasants found it messy to carry pizza out into the fields for lunch, so some enterprising cook came up with the idea of folding the pizza in half and cooking it that way.

½ **cup ricotta**

½ **cup shredded mozzarella**

¼ **cup grated Parmesan cheese**

¼ **cup chopped grilled ham (page 305)**

**Puree from 8 cloves Caramelized Garlic (page 302)**

**1 teaspoon dried basil**

**1 teaspoon dried oregano**

½ **teaspoon hot red pepper flakes (optional)**

**2 pizza discs (page 304)**

**Olive oil**

**P**reheat the grill.

**I**n a medium bowl combine the ricotta, mozzarella, Parmesan cheese, ham, garlic, basil, oregano, and optional pepper flakes and mix well. Divide the pizza dough in half and roll each out on a lightly floured surface into 6-inch discs. Place half the cheese mixture on the bottom half of each disc. Make a turnover by folding the top half of the dough down. Seal the edges by pressing them together with the tines of a fork.

**B**rush the calzones with olive oil and place on the grill for 8 to 10 minutes. Brush the tops with more oil, turn, and grill 8 to 10 minutes longer. If you tap the cooked dough, it should sound hollow.

# Pork Tenderloin with Garlic and Red Pepper Pesto

**Makes 4 servings**

**P**ork tenderloins are as popular in supermarkets today as pork chops. They're a little more expensive, but there is no waste and they are very lean. Avoid overcooking because they dry out very easily.

**2 pork tenderloin fillets**

**1 cup Garlic and Red Pepper Pesto (recipe follows)**

**T**rim any fat from the tenderloins and remove silver skin. Rub the meat with ¾ cup of the pesto and refrigerate overnight.

**P**reheat the grill.

**P**lace the tenderloins on the grill and sear on all sides over high heat, about 8 to 10 minutes. Move the meat to medium heat and continue cooking for 5 to 6 minutes, or until done. Remove from the grill and set the meat aside for 5 minutes before cutting on the diagonal into thin slices. Arrange the slices on a platter and top with the remaining pesto.

*Grill temperature*

**high, then medium**

*Summer Menu 13*

(continued)

# Garlic and Red Pepper Pesto

## Makes about 1 1/2 cups

**Puree from 1 head Caramelized Garlic (page 302)**

**1/4 cup pine nuts**

**3/4 cup grilled (page 303) and peeled red chili peppers**

**2 to 3 grilled (page 303) and peeled jalapeño peppers**

**1/4 cup grated Parmesan cheese**

**1/4 cup olive oil**

Place the garlic and pine nuts in the bowl of a food processor and process for 10 seconds. Add the red pepper and jalapeños and process for 20 seconds. Add the cheese and process for 10 seconds. With the motor going, slowly add the olive oil.

# Plum Tart

**Makes 6 to 8 servings**

*Grill temperature*

**medium**

**I** find a lot of people don't like to eat plums out of hand, but are surprised to find them totally different when cooked. Any juicy ripe plum can be used in this tart. Try Italian prune plums, which can be pitted rather easily.

**Pastry for an 8-inch tart**

**2 pints plums, cut in half and pitted**

**½ cup granulated sugar**

**3 tablespoons butter, at room temperature, cut into small pieces**

**1 teaspoon ground cinnamon**

**1 teaspoon vanilla extract**

**2 tablespoons all-purpose flour**

**Confectioners' sugar**

**P**reheat the grill.

**F**it the pastry into the tart shell and arrange the plums on top. In a small bowl combine the sugar, butter, cinnamon, and vanilla. Add the flour and rub the ingredients together with your fingertips or a fork until the mixture forms coarse crumbs. Scatter this crumb mixture over the plums and sprinkle with confectioners' sugar. Place on a raised shelf in the grill, lower the hood, and bake for 30 to 35 minutes. Cool slightly and sprinkle with additional confectioners' sugar.

*Summer Menu 13*

# Menu 14

*Soft-Shell Crab Sandwich*

*Caramelized Garlic Dip*

*Barbecued Portobello Mushrooms*

*Carrot Slaw*

*Pennsylvania Chicken Pot Pie*

*Spiced Cherries*

We tend to forget the unsung heroes. They rarely make the newspapers and we don't see them on the evening news, but we know we can count on them when there's an emergency. Celebrate all the professional service people of the community—firefighters, police officers, doctors, nurses, EMS technicians—who perform their craft well and make our communities safer and better places to grill.

# Soft-Shell Crab Sandwich

**Makes 4 servings**

*Grill temperature*

**high**

**I**always look forward to soft-shell crab sandwiches from May to September, when they're in season. You can buy them frozen, but somehow they just don't taste the same. "Soft shell" refers to the few days between when a crab sheds its old shell as part of its growth cycle and when the new one hardens.

> ¼ **cup olive oil**
>
> **Puree from 1 head Caramelized Garlic (page 302)**
>
> **Juice of 2 lemons**
>
> **2 teaspoons Tabasco**
>
> **8 large soft-shell crabs, cleaned**
>
> **8 slices sourdough bread**
>
> **Caramelized Garlic Dip (recipe follows)**

**C**ombine the olive oil, garlic, lemon juice, and Tabasco in a shallow bowl and mix well. Add the crabs and marinate, refrigerated, for 30 minutes.

**P**reheat the grill.

**R**emove the crabs from the marinade and grill 2 minutes on each side. Grill the sourdough bread until grill marks appear, about 30 seconds on each side. Brush the bread with the dip and make 4 sandwiches using 2 crabs for each.

# Caramelized Garlic Dip

**Makes about 1 cup**

**U**se as a dip with crudités, grilled bread, tortillas, or pita bread. It also works well as a dressing for fish.

½ cup sour cream
½ cup plain yogurt or mayonnaise
Puree from 1 head Caramelized Garlic (page 302)
2 tablespoons grated Parmesan cheese
Juice of ½ lemon
½ teaspoon paprika
½ teaspoon Tabasco
½ teaspoon dry mustard

**I**n a small bowl combine the sour cream, yogurt, garlic, cheese, lemon juice, paprika, Tabasco, and dry mustard and blend well. Chill 1 hour before using.

*Summer*
*Menu 14*

**135**

# Barbecued Portobello Mushrooms

### Makes 4 servings

*Grill temperature*

**high, then medium**

**W**hen Portobello mushrooms first came on the market just a few years ago, they were considered simply overgrown mushrooms, but because of their texture and meatiness, they soon became a steak substitute for vegetarians and those who wanted to cut down on red meat. Here I've taken the Portobello mushroom and given it the good ol' barbecue treatment.

**4 Portobello mushrooms**

**Puree from 1 head Caramelized Garlic (page 302)**

**½ teaspoon dried thyme**

**½ teaspoon dried rosemary, crumbled**

**¼ cup olive oil**

**¼ cup balsamic vinegar**

**¼ cup chopped scallions**

**2 tablespoons catsup**

**1 tablespoon honey**

**1 teaspoon soy sauce**

**Freshly ground black pepper**

*Gather 'Round the Grill*

**C**ut off the mushroom stems, wash lightly, chop, and set aside. Rinse the caps, if necessary. Rub them with the garlic, sprinkle with thyme and rosemary, and drizzle with olive oil.

136

**T**o make the sauce combine the chopped mushroom stems, balsamic vinegar, scallions, catsup, honey, soy sauce, and black pepper in a small saucepan on the stovetop or side burner and bring to a boil. Lower heat, and simmer 4 to 5 minutes.

**P**reheat the grill.

**G**rill the mushrooms, caps down, for 2 to 3 minutes on a very hot grill. Turn and cook 2 minutes longer, over medium heat, basting with the sauce. Serve extra sauce on the side.

# Carrot Slaw

**Makes 6 to 8 servings**

**C**arrots have an indefinite shelf life, but try to find those that are fairly fresh. Don't be afraid to taste the carrot before mixing up the recipe, so you can adjust the sweetness accordingly. The carrots can be shredded by hand using a four-sided grater or in a food processor.

1 thick slice fresh pineapple, grilled (page 305), cut into chunks

1 small onion, sliced and grilled (page 303), chopped

6 scallions, grilled (page 303) and cut into 2-inch pieces on an angle

4 cups peeled and shredded carrots

½ cup finely shredded red cabbage

1 cup pineapple juice

Puree from 8 cloves Caramelized Garlic (page 302)

½ cup sugar

1 tablespoon cider vinegar

1 teaspoon Tabasco

½ teaspoon ground cumin

½ teaspoon ground coriander

Freshly ground black pepper to taste

¼ cup toasted or smoked pecans

**I**n a large bowl combine the grilled pineapple, onion, scallions, carrots, and red cabbage. In a separate bowl combine the pineapple juice, garlic, sugar, vinegar, Tabasco, cumin, coriander, and black pepper. Pour the dressing over the vegetables and toss lightly. Chill 2 hours. Garnish with toasted pecans.

# Pennsylvania Chicken Pot Pie

**Makes 4 servings**

Grill
temperature
**medium**

This pot pie is called "Pennsylvania," in honor of the Pennsylvania Dutch, because it's topped with noodles rather than a biscuit crust. This is a good way to use up leftover chicken (or even turkey). You can include leftover potatoes, string beans, or any other appropriate vegetable.

> 1½ pounds boneless and skinless chicken breasts
>
> 2 tablespoons butter
>
> 1 medium onion, thickly sliced, grilled (page 303), and diced
>
> 1 cup grilled (page 303) and sliced white mushrooms
>
> 2 ribs celery, diced
>
> 2 carrots, peeled and diced
>
> 2 tablespoons all-purpose flour
>
> 2 cups chicken stock
>
> ½ cup peas (fresh or frozen)
>
> 3 bay leaves
>
> Pinch ground nutmeg
>
> 2 cups cooked wide egg noodles

Preheat the grill.

Grill the chicken breasts 4 to 5 minutes on each side. Remove, cool, and slice into 1-inch pieces.

Heat the butter in a large saucepan on a side burner. Add the onion, mushrooms, celery, and carrots and simmer 2 to 3 minutes. Stir in the flour and cook 2 to 3

Summer
Menu 14

minutes longer, stirring constantly. Slowly add the chicken stock, peas, bay leaves, nutmeg, and grilled chicken pieces. Bring the mixture to a boil, reduce the heat, and place in an ovenproof dish. Top with cooked noodles and heat the dish over medium heat, with the cover down, on the grill for 5 minutes.

# Spiced Cherries

**Makes 4 servings**

*Grill temperature*

**medium-high**

**C**herries are in season from May until August. Buy only those that are firm, shiny, and plump. Serve these boozy cherries warm over sponge cake or ice cream.

> ½ **cup sugar**
>
> 1 **tablespoon butter**
>
> 2 **cups pitted cherries**
>
> ¼ **cup orange juice**
>
> ¼ **teaspoon ground cinnamon**
>
> **Pinch ground allspice**
>
> ¼ **cup brandy**
>
> **Sponge cake or vanilla ice cream**

*Gather 'Round the Grill*

**P**reheat the grill.

**I**n a heavy saucepan on the grill, combine the sugar and butter and cook until they melt. Add the cherries and simmer 2 minutes. Add the orange juice, cinnamon, and allspice and simmer 2 minutes longer. Warm the brandy and add it to the cherries. Carefully tilt the pan, igniting the brandy, and let the alcohol burn off. Serve over sponge cake or vanilla ice cream.

# Menu 15

*Con Queso*

*Grilled Salsa*

*Sausage-Stuffed Potatoes*

*Chilled Avocado Soup*

*Ceviche-Style Swordfish on Skewers*

*Beef Fajitas with Guacamole*

*Caramel Fondue*

San Antonio is part Old World and, most certainly, part New World. Lunch hour is apt to be a long one, however, dating back to pre–air-conditioned days when the custom was to take a two-hour siesta. When it's summertime, the living should be easy. And it's just as easy to find something to celebrate—like opening the pool for the season or putting the boat in the water. Or just taking a stroll along the River Walk—the Paseo del Rió— San Antonio's answer to the canals of Venice.

# Con Queso

**Makes about 4 cups**

**C**on queso means "with cheese" and this recipe makes a great dip for chunks of warm grilled tortillas. You can also use it as a filling for quesadillas or as a sauce over grilled chicken or firm grilled fin fish such as halibut, monkfish, cod, or even shrimp or scallops.

> **3 cups shredded Cheddar cheese (about 12 ounces)**
> **8 ounces cream cheese, cut into pieces, at room temperature**
> **½ cup heavy cream**
> **2 cups Grilled Salsa (recipe follows)**

**P**reheat the grill.

**I**n a large saucepan on the grill, combine the Cheddar cheese, cream cheese, and heavy cream. Melt slowly over low heat. Slowly add the salsa, stirring constantly, and serve warm.

# Grilled Salsa

**Makes 2 cups**

**G**rilling the vegetables first gives this salsa a unique smoky flavor.

*Grill temperature*

**medium-high**

10 plum tomatoes, grilled (page 303)

6 scallions, grilled (page 303)

1 green bell pepper, grilled (page 302)

3 jalapeño peppers, grilled (page 303)

Puree from 2 cloves Caramelized Garlic (page 302)

Juice and zest of 1 lime

¼ cup chopped fresh cilantro

Salt and pepper to taste

Tabasco to taste

**R**emove the seeds from the peppers and chop the vegetables. In a medium bowl combine the vegetables with the garlic, lime juice and zest, cilantro, salt, pepper, and Tabasco. Stir well and set aside for 1 hour before serving to allow the flavors to meld.

*Summer Menu 15*

# Sausage-Stuffed Potatoes

### Makes 4 servings

*Grill temperature*

**medium, then high**

**S**omehow whenever I grill there are always sausages or potatoes leftover, and that's how this recipe actually came about. A little bit left on the left and a little bit left on the right and when the two are mixed together, it becomes an excellent second-day dish the whole family will enjoy.

**4 large russet potatoes, baked on grill (page 303) and cooled**

**½ pound hot Italian sausage, grilled (page 305) and cooled**

**½ cup ricotta**

**2 tablespoons bread crumbs**

**2 tablespoons grated Parmesan cheese**

**1 tablespoon chopped fresh Italian parsley**

**C**ut an oblong section from the top of each potato and scoop out the pulp with a soup spoon, leaving a ¼-inch rim so that the potato holds it shape. Remove the sausage meat from its casing. In a medium bowl combine the potato pulp, sausage, ricotta, bread crumbs, Parmesan cheese, and parsley and mix well. Stuff the potatoes evenly with the sausage mixture.

**P**reheat the grill.

**C**ook the potatoes on the grill over medium heat for 5 to 7 minutes, then on high for 1 to 2 minutes. Serve immediately.

# Chilled Avocado Soup

**S**erve this soup with a dollop of sour cream and sprinkle on grilled tortilla croutons, chopped scallions, and bacon bits. The soup makes a good first course if you're planning on grilled chicken, shrimp, or scallops.

- 4 ripe avocados
- Juice of 3 limes
- 1 large tomato, grilled (page 303) and chopped
- 1 bunch scallions, grilled (page 303) and chopped
- Puree from 1 head Caramelized Garlic (page 302)
- 2 cups chicken stock
- 2 tablespoons chopped fresh cilantro
- 2 ounces (¼ cup) tequila
- ½ teaspoon Tabasco

**P**eel the avocados and remove the pits. Cut 3 avocados into chunks and puree with the lime juice in a blender or food processor. Place the puree into a bowl.

**C**oarsely chop the remaining avocado. Stir the chopped avocado, tomato, scallions, garlic, chicken stock, cilantro, tequila, and Tabasco into the pureed avocado and mix until well blended. Cover and chill ½ hour and serve immediately.

*Summer*
*Menu 15*

# Ceviche-Style Swordfish on Skewers

## Makes 4 servings

**C**eviche is raw fish "cooked" in lime juice, but here it serves as a marinade for the swordfish before it's grilled. Thinly sliced yellow squash and green zucchini grilled on separate skewers go nicely with the swordfish.

> **Juice of 2 limes**
>
> **2 ounces (¼ cup) tequila**
>
> **1 teaspoon red pepper flakes**
>
> **1 teaspoon chopped fresh cilantro**
>
> **1 pound swordfish, cut into 1-inch cubes**
>
> **1 tablespoon olive oil**

**I**n a shallow bowl combine the lime juice, tequila, red pepper flakes, and cilantro. Add the swordfish and marinate 2 hours in the refrigerator.

**P**reheat the grill.

**R**emove the swordfish from the marinade and thread on skewers. Brush the fish with olive oil and sear for 30 to 45 seconds on each side. Remove immediately and serve.

# Beef Fajitas with Guacamole

## Makes 4 servings

**F**ajitas are traditionally made with skirt steak marinated for 24 hours and then grilled. Shrimp, chicken, or pork marinated for about 2 hours can be substituted for the beef and is every bit as delicious. The colors of the dish, from the salsa and red and green peppers to the guacamole and sour cream, make this a festive dish worthy of any celebration.

> **2½-pound beef skirt steak, trimmed**
> **Fajita Marinade (recipe follows)**
> **8 flour tortillas**
> **Grilled Salsa (page 143)**
> **3 green or red bell peppers, grilled (page 302), seeded, and sliced**
> **2 large onions, thickly sliced, grilled (page 303) and chopped**
> **4 plum tomatoes, split, grilled (page 303), and chopped**
> **Guacamole (page 149)**
> **Sour cream**

**M**arinate the steak in the marinade for 24 hours in the refrigerator, turning occasionally.

**P**reheat the grill.

**R**emove the steak from the marinade and grill for 3 to 4 minutes on each side, continuously basting with the marinade. Remove from grill and slice on the diagonal.

**D**ivide the meat among the tortillas and garnish with the Grilled Salsa, grilled peppers and onions, grilled tomatoes, Guacamole, and sour cream.

*Grill temperature*
**high, then**

*Summer Menu 15*

*(continued)*

# Fajita Marinade

**Makes about 1³/₄ cups**

½ cup lime juice (about 4 limes)

½ cup olive oil

4 ounces (½ cup) tequila

1 tablespoon Worcestershire sauce

1 teaspoon Tabasco

1 teaspoon chopped fresh cilantro

½ teaspoon ground cumin

Combine all ingredients in a nonreactive bowl and mix well.

# Guacamole

**Makes 4 servings**

3 ripe avocados

1 large tomato, grilled (page 303), seeded, and chopped

Puree from 4 cloves Caramelized Garlic (page 302)

Juice of 1 lime

2 tablespoons chopped fresh cilantro

Red pepper flakes to taste

Salt and pepper to taste

**P**eel the avocados, cut them in half, and remove the pits. Cut the avocados into small chunks and place in a nonreactive bowl. Add the tomato, garlic, lime juice, cilantro, red pepper flakes, salt, and pepper. Mix well, cover, and refrigerate for at least 1 hour for flavors to meld.

*Summer*
*Menu 15*

# Caramel Fondue

**Makes 4 servings**

**P**lace the fondue in the center of the table and give everyone a long-handled fondue fork. Place bowls of cut-up apples, pears, bananas, peaches, and sponge cake around and let everyone dip their own.

> 1½ **cups sugar**
> **Juice and zest of** ½ **lemon**
> 3 **tablespoons butter**
> ¼ **cup heavy cream**

**P**reheat the grill.

**I**n a medium heavy-duty saucepan combine the sugar, lemon juice, and zest and heat the mixture on the grill, stirring constantly. At first the sugar will look like wet sand, but after 2 minutes or so, it will melt into a clear liquid and eventually turn amber. At this point add the butter and let the mixture simmer for a minute or so. Add the cream, bring to a boil, and cook 2 minutes. Be careful; the caramel will be very hot. Remove from the heat and allow to cool slightly.

*Gather*
*'Round*
*the*
*Grill*

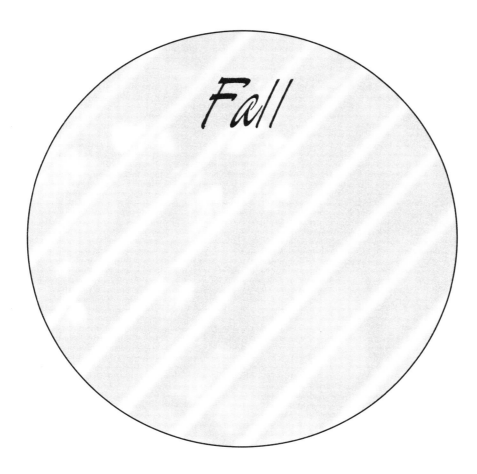

Fall

# Menu 16

*Hot-Smoked Pumpkin Seeds*

*Corn and White Bean Soup*

*Broccoli and Lemon with Grilled Peppers*

*Pumpkin Stuffed with Chicken and Rice*

*Cinnamon Apple Burritos*

Living close to the farming community on the East End of Long Island has certain advantages: there are wonderful field-ripened strawberries, fresh-picked corn on the cob, and come August, real tomatoes. In the fall, the leaves turn to autumn colors, the days meld into Indian summer, and a huge golden moon smiles over the fields. It's time to get together with those we love and commemorate the harvest.

# Hot-Smoked Pumpkin Seeds

**Makes 4 to 6 servings**

**O**nce you've cut into your pumpkin, the seeds are a bonus. Rather than discard them, Toss some of them on the grill while you're preparing the rest of the meal.

> **Wood chips (hickory, apple, mesquite)**
> **Seeds from 1 large pumpkin (about 2 cups)**
> **1 tablespoon olive oil**
> **1 tablespoon melted margarine**
> **Salt to taste**

**P**repare an iron smoker box.

**S**oak the wood chips in water for 20 minutes. Drain off the water, place the chips in the smoker box, and place the box on a corner of the grate.

**R**emove and discard the strings from the pumpkin seeds. Rinse the seeds under cool water and pat dry.

**C**ombine the olive oil, margarine, and pumpkin seeds and toss well. Place in a disposable foil pan or skillet on the grill. Cook until they turn light brown, about 10 to 15 minutes, stirring frequently. Remove the seeds and sprinkle with salt to taste.

**H**ere are some suggestions for varying the flavor of your pumpkin seeds. Add the flavorings when you salt the seeds.

Italian—add ½ teaspoon oregano

Southwestern—add ½ teaspoon chili powder

Caribbean—add ½ teaspoon curry powder
Sweet twist—omit the salt; add 1 tablespoon granulated sugar,
  ½ teaspoon ground cinnamon, and a pinch of ground nutmeg

# Corn and White Bean Soup

**Makes 4 to 6 servings**

Grill
temperature

**medium-
low**

Here's a soup that gives you several options. As is, the grilled corn and onion impart a smoky flavor to the beans and potatoes. For a richer flavor, you can add a cup of light or heavy cream at the end, or you can stir in 1 teaspoon chopped cilantro and ½ teaspoon ground cumin to give it a Southwestern taste. Whichever way you go, it's a hearty fall dish.

**4 ears corn**

**1 medium onion, sliced in rings**

**1 tablespoon olive oil**

**1 cup white beans, such as navy or pea beans, soaked in water overnight**

**8 cups chicken stock**

**1 medium potato, peeled and diced**

**1 teaspoon Tabasco**

**2 bay leaves**

**½ teaspoon dried thyme**

**½ cup diced fresh tomato**

**1 tablespoon chopped fresh parsley**

*Fall
Menu 16*

(continued)

155

**P**reheat the grill.

**L**ightly brush the corn and onion slices with the olive oil and grill over medium-low heat until light brown. Cut the kernels from the cobs and cut the onion into ½-inch pieces.

**D**rain the water from the beans and place in a large stockpot with the chicken stock, corn kernels, onion, potato, Tabasco, bay leaves, and thyme. Bring to a boil, lower heat, and simmer until the beans are tender, 45 to 50 minutes. Discard the bay leaves.

**P**uree three fourths of the soup in a blender or food processor and return to the pot. Reheat the soup and stir in the tomato and parsley.

# Broccoli and Lemon with Grilled Peppers

**Makes 4 to 6 servings**

**B**roccoli is one of the healthiest vegetables around, having twice the vitamin C in an orange and nearly as much calcium as milk. And you can't beat the flavor of local emerald-green broccoli.

For a very special taste, sprinkle the salad with smoked pecans, walnuts, or hazelnuts or some hulled pumpkin seeds just before serving.

> **1 head broccoli**
> **Puree from 1 head Caramelized Garlic (page 302)**
> **½ cup olive oil**
> **Juice of 3 lemons**
> **4 large red bell peppers, cut into 1-inch strips, grilled (page 302)**
> **Freshly ground black pepper**

**P**reheat the grill.

**W**ash the broccoli and cut off the florets. Peel the stems and slice into ½-inch rounds. Drop the broccoli into salted boiling water and cook on the grill until crisp-tender, about 3 minutes. Drain immediately in a colander and run the broccoli under cold water.

**W**hisk the garlic puree with the olive oil and lemon juice until well blended.

**I**n a large serving bowl combine the broccoli and red pepper. Pour the dressing over the vegetables, sprinkle with black pepper, and toss gently. Allow the salad to marinate for 1 hour before serving.

# Pumpkin Stuffed with Chicken and Rice

### Makes 4 servings

The ultimate one-dish meal is cooked in its own pot—in this case it's a pumpkin. I remember the year we picked a lot of pumpkins for decoration at my restaurant on Long Island. When it came time to use them up, this dish became a very popular item on the menu.

If you like to experiment, toss in some cannellini beans, chickpeas, or slices of smoked sausage when you add the chicken.

> **2 large pumpkins (8 to 12 inches in diameter)**
>
> **One 3-pound chicken, cut into 8 pieces, or 1½ pounds chicken cutlets**
>
> **2 tablespoons olive oil**
>
> **½ medium onion, cut into rings**
>
> **1 large red bell pepper, seeded and cut into 1-inch strips**
>
> **1 cup Converted rice**
>
> **2 cups chicken or vegetable stock**
>
> **Puree from 1 head Caramelized Garlic (page 302)**
>
> **2 bay leaves**
>
> **2 tablespoons chopped fresh cilantro**
>
> **1 teaspoon Tabasco**
>
> **½ cup chopped tomatoes**

**P**reheat the grill.

**U**sing a sharp knife, cut a 5-inch hole in the top of the pumpkin and remove the seeds. Reserve the lid.

**B**rush the chicken with some of the olive oil and grill about 20 minutes or until three-fourths done. (If using cutlets, grill 4 to 5 minutes.) Brush the onion and red pepper with the remaining olive oil and grill until light brown, about 4 to 5 minutes.

**I**n a large saucepan heat the rice and stock. Add the garlic, bay leaves, cilantro, Tabasco, and tomatoes. When the mixture begins to boil, stir in the onion, red bell pepper, and the par-cooked chicken.

**W**rap the bottom of the pumpkin with foil. Spoon the mixture into the pumpkin, then cover with the pumpkin lid. Place the pumpkin on the grill, lower the grill hood, and cook 45 to 50 minutes. Remove the pumpkin from the grill, discarding aluminum foil and bay leaves.

**A**dd a little additional stock if the mixture is too dry. Bring the pumpkin to the table and serve the chicken directly from it.

*Fall*
*Menu 16*

# Cinnamon Apple Burritos

### Makes 6 servings

*Grill temperature*

**low-medium**

**W**hen you're out picking pumpkins, find out if there's a spot nearby where you can pick apples for this simple, but delicious, fall dessert. If you want to gild the lily, add a scoop of vanilla ice cream or a dollop of whipped cream on top of each serving.

> **6 baking apples, such as Rome, Greening, or McIntosh,**
>    **peeled, cored, and halved**
> **6 tablespoons melted butter**
> **1 cup granulated sugar**
> **2 teaspoons ground cinnamon**
> **Juice of 1 lemon**
> **Six 10-inch flour tortillas**
> **Cinnamon sugar**

**P**reheat the grill or side burner.

**B**rush the apple halves with 2 tablespoons of the melted butter, grill 2 to 3 minutes on each side, and coarsely chop.

**H**eat 2 tablespoons of the butter in a saucepan on the grill or side burner. Add the apples, sugar, and cinnamon and cook until the apples are tender and syrupy. Stir in the lemon juice and cool.

**L**ay the flour tortillas on a flat surface and spoon an equal amount of the filling in the center of each. Fold up the bottom, fold in the sides, and roll up from the bottom, similar to rolling an egg roll. Brush the tortillas with the remaining 2 tablespoons butter and heat them on the grill until the filling is hot and the tortillas are crisp. Remove and sprinkle with cinnamon sugar.

# Menu 17

Linguine with Squid

Steak Salad

Chive Potato Pancakes

Deviled Cod

Grilled Peach Pizza

Our first cities were settled on the banks of rivers because they provided easy transportation. Even today, a city on "a river with a view" will use it as a background for parks, apartments, shopping areas, and dining because it enhances the surroundings. What can be better than our natural environment? Sometimes we have to stop and smell the roses or, in this case, the water, the trees, and the skies.

# Linguine with Squid

**Makes 4 servings**

*Grill temperature*

**high, then low**

**S**ome like it hot, and you can give them what they want by sprinkling the calamari with red pepper flakes before grilling. If you're a seafood lover, add a few grilled shrimp, clams, and scallops to the sauce.

**1 pound linguine**

**4 tablespoons olive oil**

**2 pounds calamari, cleaned and cut into rings**

**3 cups Grilled Tomato Sauce (page 290)**

**½ cup dry red wine**

**Puree from 6 cloves Caramelized Garlic (page 302)**

**1 teaspoon Tabasco**

**O**n the stovetop, cook the linguine until al dente. Drain well, place in a serving bowl, and toss with 2 tablespoons olive oil. Keep warm while preparing the sauce.

**P**reheat the grill.

**B**rush the calamari with the remaining 2 tablespoons olive oil and toss onto hot grill for 2 minutes, turning once.

**I**n a large saucepan combine the tomato sauce, wine, garlic, and Tabasco and heat over low heat until it is simmering. Add the squid and stir well. Pour the sauce over the linguine, toss well, and serve immediately.

*Gather 'Round the Grill*

# Steak Salad

## Makes 8 servings

Stretch the meat budget by taking the New York Strip Steak recipe and cutting the meat into strips, using it in a salad, and thereby cutting down on calories as well as cholesterol.

*Grill temperature*

**high**

**1 recipe New York Strip Steak (page 20)**

**2 heads red leaf or romaine lettuce, washed and dried**

**1 cup croutons**

**½ cup grated Parmesan cheese (optional)**

**1 cup Steak Dressing (recipe follows)**

**Freshly ground black pepper**

Grill the steaks, remove from grill, and allow to rest 5 minutes. With a sharp knife, cut into ¼-inch strips.

Arrange the greens on a large serving platter. Arrange the sliced steak on the lettuce and top with croutons and Parmesan cheese. Pour the dressing over the salad and add a few grindings of fresh pepper.

*(continued)*

*Fall Menu 17*

# Steak Dressing

### Makes about 2 1/2 cups

**C**ut down on the calories by using low-fat mayonnaise and fat-free yogurt.

> **2 cups mayonnaise**
> **4 ounces plain yogurt**
> **Puree from 8 cloves Caramelized Garlic (page 302)**
> **Juice of 2 lemons**
> **2 tablespoons spicy steak sauce**
> **2 tablespoons finely chopped fresh cilantro**

**C**ombine all the ingredients in a nonreactive bowl and mix well.

# Chive Potato Pancakes

## Makes 4 servings

**A**ssemble the ingredients just before cooking. If you prefer a lower-calorie pancake, use a nonstick pan and a vegetable cooking spray.

*Grill temperature*

**medium**

**3 medium russet potatoes**

**⅓ cup all-purpose flour**

**¼ cup grated raw onion**

**¼ cup chopped fresh chives**

**Puree from 2 cloves Caramelized Garlic (page 302)**

**½ teaspoon baking powder**

**¼ teaspoon Tabasco**

**Pinch ground nutmeg**

**Freshly ground black pepper**

**2 eggs, lightly beaten**

**Vegetable oil, for frying**

**P**reheat the grill.

**C**oarsely grate the potatoes into a large bowl. Add the flour, onion, chive, garlic, baking powder, Tabasco, nutmeg, and black pepper and mix well. Add the eggs and blend well. Heat a heavy skillet on the grill and fill with oil to ¼ inch. For each pancake drop ¼ cup of the potato mixture in the fat and cook until golden on both sides, approximately 5 to 6 minutes.

*Fall*
*Menu 17*

# Deviled Cod

**Makes 4 servings**

*Grill temperature*

**high-medium**

**C**od is available in most parts of the country year-round. It's a hearty fish that is abundant especially during the colder months when many fishermen aren't venturing out because most fish have migrated to warmer waters. The neutral flavor of cod holds up well to the spicy seasonings in the topping.

> **Four 12-inch squares heavy-duty foil**
> **2 tablespoons melted margarine**
> **1½ to 2 pounds cod fillets, cut into 4 pieces**
> **¼ cup Dijon mustard**
> **1 tablespoon capers, rinsed and drained**
> **1 tablespoon chopped Italian parsley**
> **Juice of 1 lemon**
> **1 to 2 teaspoons Tabasco**
> **Freshly ground black pepper**

**P**reheat the grill.

**B**rush the foil with some of the melted margarine. Place a piece of cod in the center of each piece of foil and brush with the remaining margarine. In a small bowl combine the Dijon mustard, capers, parsley, lemon juice, and Tabasco and mix well. Spread the mixture evenly on the fish and sprinkle with pepper. Loosely enclose the fish in the foil and grill for 8 to 10 minutes. Do not overcook the cod.

*Gather 'Round the Grill*

# Grilled Peach Pizza

## Makes 4 servings

Grill
temperature
**medium**

**D**on't be afraid to sprinkle a lot of cinnamon sugar on the grilled dough; if you eat them at this point, it will be like biting into doughnuts. Mascarpone is a thick, creamy Italian cheese somewhat like cream cheese but with a slight tang. If you can't find it, substitute 5 tablespoons cream cheese and 3 tablespoons sour cream for the ½ cup mascarpone.

> **4 to 5 ripe peaches, split and pitted, or frozen peaches, defrosted**
> **and patted dry**
> **2 pizza discs (page 304)**
> **¼ cup melted butter**
> **¼ teaspoon cinnamon sugar**
> **½ cup mascarpone**
> **6 fresh mint leaves**

**P**reheat the grill.

**P**lace the peaches on the grill, cut side down, and grill for 2 to 3 minutes. Remove, cool slightly, and slice.

**R**oll out the pizza dough on a lightly floured surface into two 6-inch discs. Brush both sides with butter and place on the grill for 2 to 3 minutes. Remove, brush again with butter, and grill until fully cooked, about 5 to 7 minutes. (They will have a hollow sound when tapped.) Brush again with butter and sprinkle heavily with cinnamon sugar on both sides. Spread with the mascarpone and top with grilled peach slices. Garnish with the mint leaves.

Fall
Menu 17

# Menu 18

*Maryland Crab Cakes*

*Grilled Papaya Salad with Shrimp and*

*Maui Onion Vinaigrette*

*Mahimahi with Fresh Ginger and Lime*

*Pineapple Kabobs*

When we think of the paradise called Polynesia, we think of hula dancers, palm trees, and a luau—the traditional Hawaiian feast centered around a roasted pig. Well, we're having too much fun to spend ten to twelve hours waiting for the food to cook. We propose a simpler menu so there's more time to celebrate with singing and dancing. Hula, anyone?

# Maryland Crab Cakes

### Makes 4 servings

*Grill
temperature*

**low, then
medium-high**

Thse crab cakes are based on a cream sauce loaded with fresh crab meat. For a special treat, top them with a trio of sauces—grilled tomato sauce, garlic dip, and seafood sauce.

**2 tablespoons butter**

**½ medium onion, sliced, grilled (page 303), and chopped**

**½ cup chopped scallions**

**Puree from 4 cloves Caramelized Garlic (page 302)**

**1 teaspoon paprika**

**1 teaspoon Tabasco**

**½ teaspoon dried parsley**

**½ teaspoon dried basil**

**½ teaspoon dried thyme**

**2 tablespoons all-purpose flour**

**2 cups milk or half-and-half**

**1 pound lump crab meat**

**1½ cups bread crumbs made from day-old French bread**

**2 eggs, lightly beaten**

**1 cup corn flour\* or ½ cup finely ground yellow cornmeal with
    ½ cup all-purpose flour**

**¼ cup vegetable oil**

*\*Finely ground cornmeal used for breading and in combination with other flours in baking, corn flour is milled from the whole kernel and is not to be confused with masa harina. Readily available throughout the South, but more difficult to find elsewhere.*

*Gather
'Round
the
Grill*

**170**

**P**reheat the grill or side burner.

**I**n a large saucepan heat the butter over low heat on the grill. Add the onion, scallions, garlic, paprika, Tabasco, parsley, basil, and thyme and cook for 2 to 3 minutes. Stir in the flour and cook over low heat for 4 to 5 minutes, stirring frequently. Slowly whisk in the milk and blend well. Add half the crab meat and cook for 10 minutes, stirring occasionally.

**R**emove pan from the grill, stir in the bread crumbs, and cool. Stir in the eggs and mix well. Gently fold in the remaining crab meat. The mixture will be soft. Form mixture into 8 patties, about 3 inches in diameter. Lightly press together with your hands and dredge in corn flour. Refrigerate until firm or freeze.

**H**eat the vegetable oil in a sauté pan to medium-high. Place 2 refrigerated or frozen crab cakes in the hot pan, searing on each side for 4 to 5 minutes. Once they are brown, lower the heat and cook 4 to 5 minutes longer. Drain on paper towels.

# Grilled Papaya Salad with Shrimp and Maui Onion Vinaigrette

**Makes 4 servings**

This is one recipe where not just any onion will do. Maui onions grown on Maui, one of the Hawaiian Islands, are extremely sweet and mild. Vidalia onions from Georgia or Texas onions might be substituted, but if you are unable to get one of these three, use half the amount of grilled onion and increase the honey to 2 tablespoons.

**2 medium green or half-ripe papayas**
**12 medium shrimp**

### Marinade for Papaya

**Juice of 2 limes**
**2 tablespoons olive oil**
**1 tablespoon finely chopped fresh ginger**

### Marinade for Shrimp

**2 tablespoons olive oil**
**1 tablespoon lime juice**
**1 tablespoon Dijon mustard**
**1 teaspoon finely chopped fresh mint**

1 yellow and 1 red bell pepper
1 tablespoon olive oil
Lettuce leaves
Maui Onion Vinaigrette (recipe follows)

**P**reheat the grill.

**P**eel the papayas, cut in half, and remove the seeds. Peel and devein the shrimp.

**C**ombine the papaya marinade ingredients and marinate the papaya halves for 10 to 15 minutes. Combine the shrimp marinade ingredients and marinate the shrimp for 15 minutes.

**B**rush the bell peppers with the olive oil and place on the grill, turning several times until they're charred. Peel off the skins, discard the seeds, and cut peppers into 1-inch slices.

**Q**uickly sear the papaya for 1 to 2 minutes; turn and cook on the other side for another minute or so. Grill the shrimp for 2 to 3 minutes, turn, and cook on the other side for 2 to 3 minutes or until done.

**L**ine 4 salad plates with lettuce leaves. Arrange the papaya, shrimp, and peppers on top and pour the dressing over the salad.

*(continued)*

*Fall*
*Menu 18*

# Maui Onion Vinaigrette

**Makes about 2 cups**

Make this dressing a few hours before serving and do not refrigerate.

**1 medium Maui onion, sliced, grilled (page 303), and cooled**

**1 tablespoon honey**

**½ teaspoon Tabasco**

**Freshly ground black pepper to taste**

**⅓ cup balsamic vinegar**

**⅔ cup olive oil**

Place the onion, honey, Tabasco, and black pepper in a food processor or blender and process until smooth. Add the vinegar and blend well. With the motor running, slowly add the olive oil.

# Mahimahi with Fresh Ginger and Lime

**Makes 4 servings**

Grill
temperature
**high-medium**

**M**ahimahi, or dolphinfish, is not a marine mammal and should not be confused with the dolphin. Its weight averages 6 to 14 pounds and its flesh is lean with a sweet taste and a firm texture, making it ideal for smoking and grilling.

**Four 8-ounce mahimahi fillets**

**½ cup Mahimahi Marinade (recipe follows)**

**¼ cup dry white wine**

**2 tablespoons butter**

**2 tablespoons finely chopped scallions**

**1 tablespoon cracked black peppercorns**

**M**arinate the fillets in the marinade for 30 minutes.

**P**reheat the grill.

**P**lace the fillets on the hot grill and sear 2 minutes. Remove the fillets and place in an oiled skillet or pan. Pour the remaining marinade and wine over the fish, dot with butter, and scatter the scallions and peppercorns on top. Put the skillet back on the grill for 4 to 5 minutes or until the fish turns white, indicating it's cooked. Remove the fillets to a serving dish, reduce the sauce to a glaze, and pour it over the fish.

*(continued)*

Fall
Menu 18

# Mahimahi Marinade

**Makes about ²/₃ cup**

**Juice and zest of 3 limes**
**¼ cup olive oil**
**1 tablespoon finely chopped fresh ginger**
**1 teaspoon dried thyme**
**½ teaspoon Tabasco**

Combine all the ingredients and mix well.

# Pineapple Kabobs

### Makes 4 to 6 servings

*Grill temperature*

**high**

**W**hen pineapple is grilled, the sugars caramelize and the flavor becomes quite intense. Two varieties are most common in this country: the squat Red Spanish with a reddish-golden skin grows in Florida and Puerto Rico; the more expensive Cayenne, imported from Hawaii, has a golden yellow rind. Pineapples are picked ripe and do not change color. Avoid any that have soft spots or brown leaves.

**1 ripe pineapple**

**¼ cup melted butter**

**¼ cup brown sugar**

**2 tablespoons dark rum**

**½ teaspoon ground cinnamon**

**¼ teaspoon ground allspice**

**Pinch ground nutmeg**

**P**eel the pineapple, discard the core, and cut into 1-inch chunks. In a medium bowl combine the butter, brown sugar, rum, cinnamon, allspice, and nutmeg and mix well. Add the pineapple chunks and marinate 30 minutes. Remove the pineapple from the marinade and thread onto skewers.

**P**reheat the grill.

**P**lace the kabobs on the grill and cook 3 to 4 minutes, turning once.

*Fall*
*Menu 18*

**177**

# Menu 19

*Beer Cheese Soup*

*Stuffed Onions*

*Oats and Barley Topping*

*Grilled Sirloin Steak and Beer*

*Cheesecake Tart*

Microbreweries are popping up all around the country as more and more people discover the new flavors of beers brewed on a small scale. Just as we learned to cook with wine, we find beer adds another level of tang to food, especially when used in marinades. Serve this menu while watching a ball game or after a bowling tournament. Whether the favorite team wins or loses, the meal will be a treat for everyone.

# Beer Cheese Soup

## Makes 6 to 8 servings

*Grill temperature*

**medium, then low**

**I**f you replace the beer and Gruyère with dry white wine and a sharp Cheddar, you'll have a totally different twist.

**2 tablespoons butter**

**2 large onions, thickly sliced and grilled (page 303)**

**1 leek, white part only, grilled (page 53) and chopped**

**Puree from 6 cloves Caramelized Garlic (page 302)**

**2 tablespoons all-purpose flour**

**16 ounces beer**

**6 cups chicken stock**

**1 medium potato, peeled and diced**

**2 bay leaves**

**2 cups shredded Gruyère or sharp Swiss cheese (about 8 ounces)**

**¼ teaspoon Tabasco**

**P**reheat the grill or side burner.

**H**eat the butter in a 4-quart pot over medium heat. Add the onions, leek, and garlic and sauté 2 to 3 minutes or until the onions and leek are uniformly brown in color. Stir in the flour and cook 2 minutes. Add the beer and cook 2 minutes longer. Add the stock, potato, and bay leaves and bring to a boil. Lower the heat and simmer for 20 minutes. Stir in the cheese and Tabasco and cook 2 minutes, stirring constantly, until the cheese melts and the soup is smooth. Discard bay leaves.

# Stuffed Onions

**Makes 2 to 4 servings**

Ween you're stumped about what vegetable to make, short of a traditional can of peas, give this one a go. Then, next time, try the filling in bell peppers, zucchini, or tomatoes.

*Grill temperature*

**medium-low**

    **2 large onions (5 inches in diameter)**

    **3 tablespoons olive oil**

    **½ cup chopped grilled (page 303) white mushrooms**

    **Puree from 3 cloves Caramelized Garlic (page 302)**

    **½ teaspoon dried thyme**

    **½ teaspoon dried parsley**

    **Freshly ground pepper to taste**

    **¼ cup bread crumbs**

Cut the onions in half crosswise through the core. Cut a small piece from the rounded sides so they stand straight.

Preheat the grill.

Brush the onion halves with the olive oil and grill flat side down for 3 to 4 minutes. Cool slightly, then carefully remove the inner circles of onion, leaving a nest. Chop this inner part and combine in a small bowl with the mushrooms, garlic, thyme, parsley, and black pepper. Slowly add the bread crumbs until the mixture becomes dry. Stuff the onions with this mixture. Place onions on the grill and cook 15 to 20 minutes, or until tender.

*Fall Menu 19*

# Oats and Barley Topping

### Makes about 1 cup

*Grill temperature*

**medium**

**H**ere's an interesting combination of barley and oats that can be served with soup or a green salad instead of crackers or croutons.

> ¼ **cup barley**
> ½ **cup crushed pretzels**
> ¼ **cup quick-cooking oats**
> **1 tablespoon prepared mustard**
> **Freshly ground black pepper**

**P**lace the barley in a small saucepan, cover with water, and simmer until tender, about 45 minutes.

**P**reheat the grill.

**C**ombine the barley, pretzels, oats, mustard, and black pepper in a small buttered ovenproof casserole. Place on the grill and toast 5 minutes. Cool before serving.

# Grilled Sirloin Steak and Beer

### Makes 4 servings

Grill
*temperature*

**high**

**R**ather than serve this sliced steak as part of an entree, as it is here, you might cube the meat, cook it on skewers, and serve it as an appetizer.

**One 12-ounce bottle beer**

**Puree from 6 cloves Caramelized Garlic (page 302)**

**2 tablespoons balsamic vinegar**

**2 tablespoons olive oil**

**1 teaspoon dry mustard**

**1 teaspoon Worcestershire sauce**

**½ teaspoon Tabasco**

**2 pounds sirloin steak**

**Freshly ground black pepper**

**4 tablespoons butter**

**I**n a shallow bowl combine the beer, garlic, vinegar, olive oil, mustard, Worcestershire sauce, and Tabasco and mix well. Add the steak, sprinkle liberally with black pepper, and marinate 24 hours in the refrigerator, turning occasionally.

**P**reheat the grill.

**R**emove meat from marinade and place on hot grill for 3 to 4 minutes on each side. Move to medium heat or to cooler edge of the grill and cook until done.

**P**lace the remaining marinade in a small saucepan and boil 2 minutes. Stir in the butter and heat until the butter melts.

**S**lice the steak, arrange on a platter, and pour the marinade sauce over the meat.

*Fall
Menu 19*

# Cheesecake Tart

## Makes 8 servings

**C**heesecake baked on a grill tastes just as good as the one coming out of your kitchen oven. Bake it as a 9-inch tart or use individual 3½-inch graham cracker tart shells. To make the sour cream topping, spread the warm cheesecake with 1 cup sour cream.

### For Pie Crust

**1 cup graham cracker crumbs**

**1 tablespoon light or dark brown sugar**

**4 tablespoons melted margarine**

### For Filling

**Three 8-ounce packages cream cheese, softened**

**1½ cups granulated sugar**

**3 eggs**

**1 teaspoon vanilla extract**

**½ teaspoon lemon zest**

**Pinch salt**

### For Garnish

**Fresh fruit, sweetened whipped cream, or 1 cup sour cream sweetened with ¼ cup sugar**

**P**reheat the grill.

**I**n a small bowl combine the graham cracker crumbs, brown sugar, and melted margarine and mix well. Press onto the bottom and sides of a 9-inch tart pan.

**I**n a medium bowl combine the cream cheese and sugar and mix until it is smooth and creamy without any lumps. Add the eggs, one at a time, mixing well after each addition, but do not whip the mixture. Stir in the vanilla, lemon zest, and salt. Pour the mixture into the prepared tart pan. Place the pan on an elevated rack on the grill, lower the grill hood, and bake for 35 to 40 minutes. Remove at once and cool.

**S**erve with fresh fruit, whipped cream, or sour cream topping.

*Fall*
*Menu 19*

# Menu 20

*Country Peanut Butter Soup*

*Cornbread Sticks*

*Eggplant Stuffed with Oysters*

*Chicken-Fried Steak*

*Okra and Tomatoes*

*Sweet Potato and Pecan Calzone*

At one time there were more than ten thousand riverboats steaming up and down the Mississippi. They were "traveling palaces" where people were treated like royalty and served only the finest foods. To pass the time, a passenger might engage one of the Mississippi gamblers in a game of chance and win or lose his fortune. This menu allows you to celebrate in style without having to spend all your winnings from the casino, card game, or lottery. (It also leaves you with enough money to buy extra grilling books for friends.)

# Country Peanut Butter Soup

**Makes 6 to 8 servings**

*Grill temperature*

**medium-low**

**P**eanut butter doesn't always have to come between two slices of white bread. Actually, peanut butter was presented at the 1904 St. Louis World's Fair as a health food. Peanut butter soup has always been a Southern favorite—one more way inventive cooks found to use the abundant crop.

2 tablespoons butter

1 medium onion, thickly sliced, grilled (page 303), and diced

2 ribs celery, diced

2 tablespoons all-purpose flour

6 cups chicken stock

1 cup creamy peanut butter

1 bay leaf

Pinch ground nutmeg

1 cup heavy cream

6 to 8 tablespoons chopped peanuts

**P**reheat the grill or side burner.

**H**eat the butter in a 4-quart pot, add the onion and celery, and cook gently for 2 to 3 minutes, taking care not to color the vegetables. Stir in the flour and simmer 2 minutes. Add the chicken stock and peanut butter, bay leaf, and nutmeg and simmer 20 to 25 minutes. Add the cream and heat to serving temperature. Remove the bay leaf. Sprinkle individual servings with chopped peanuts.

# Cornbread Sticks

**Makes 14 sticks**

*Grill temperature*

**medium**

**T**his cornbread can also be made in a Dutch oven or in a skillet. Either way, the pan must be preheated before the filling is poured in.

> 1¼ cups finely ground yellow cornmeal
>
> ¾ cup all-purpose flour
>
> ¼ cup sugar
>
> 2 teaspoons baking powder
>
> 1 teaspoon salt
>
> 1½ cups milk
>
> ½ cup vegetable oil
>
> 1 egg

**P**reheat the grill and a well-greased cast-iron cornstick pan.

**I**n a medium bowl combine the cornmeal, flour, sugar, baking powder, and salt and toss with a fork to combine. In a separate bowl combine the milk, oil, and egg and beat lightly with a fork. Pour the wet ingredients into the dry ingredients and mix until just combined.

**P**our the batter into the hot cornstick pan, place on grill, lower the hood, and bake 20 to 25 minutes or until a toothpick inserted in the center comes out clean.

*Fall*
*Menu 20*

# Eggplant Stuffed with Oysters

**Makes 4 servings**

*Grill temperature*

**medium, then low-medium**

Choose an eggplant with a smooth, glossy skin and avoid any with dark or brown spots. Most fish markets sell shucked oysters.

> **2 medium eggplants, about 1 to ¼ pounds each**
>
> **2 cups shucked oysters, drained**
>
> **1 large onion, thickly sliced, grilled (page 303), and diced**
>
> **½ cup grilled and sliced mushrooms (page 303)**
>
> **½ cup finely chopped day-old bread**
>
> **¼ cup diced celery**
>
> **2 eggs, lightly beaten**
>
> **3 scallions, grilled (page 303) and chopped**
>
> **2 tablespoons chopped fresh Italian parsley**
>
> **½ teaspoon Worcestershire sauce**
>
> **Salt and pepper to taste**

Preheat the grill.

Lay the eggplants horizontally on a flat surface and cut a small slice from the bottom of each so that they won't roll. Cut another slice from the top of each and hollow out the eggplants, leaving 1-inch shells.

*Gather 'Round the Grill*

In a medium bowl mix the eggplant pulp, oysters, onion, mushrooms, bread, celery, eggs, scallions, parsley, Worcestershire sauce, salt, and pepper. Stuff the eggplants with this filling and place on a medium grill for 12 to 15 minutes. Move to low-medium heat for an additional 12 to 15 minutes. Do not overcook or the oysters will become tough.

# Chicken-Fried Steak

**Makes 4 servings**

Chicken-fried steak is neither chicken nor steak, but rather a tasty way to cook an inexpensive piece of beef, served with country gravy. The meat is pounded very thin to tenderize it, then breaded and fried. Every diner and country restaurant in the South and Midwest has its own version.

**2 pounds bottom round, cut into 4 pieces and pounded very thin**

**¼ cup plus 2 tablespoons all-purpose flour**

**3 eggs, lightly beaten**

**2 tablespoons milk**

**Dash each of sweet paprika, ground nutmeg, garlic powder, dried parsley, and Tabasco**

**¼ cup dry bread crumbs**

**¼ cup yellow cornmeal**

**4 tablespoons vegetable oil**

**½ grilled onion (page 303), chopped**

**1 cup chicken stock**

**½ cup half-and-half**

**½ teaspoon Tabasco**

**P**reheat the grill or side burner.

**D**redge the steak in ¼ cup flour. Mix in a shallow dish the eggs, milk, paprika, nutmeg, garlic powder, parsley, and Tabasco. In another shallow dish combine the bread crumbs and cornmeal. Dip the steaks into the egg mixture and then into the bread crumb mixture.

*(continued)*

Heat the oil in a skillet on the grill and cook the steaks 2 to 3 minutes on each side for medium or 1 minute longer on each side for well done. Remove the steaks and keep warm.

Add the onion and remaining 2 tablespoons flour to the skillet and cook 2 minutes, stirring constantly. Whisk in the chicken stock and bring to a boil. Add the half-and-half and Tabasco and simmer 2 to 3 minutes. Pour the gravy over the steaks and serve immediately.

# *Okra and Tomatoes*

**Makes 4 to 6 servings**

Okra is best known in the South, where it's often used as a thickener in dishes like gumbo. The green, finger-shaped pods are about 3 inches long. If you can't find fresh okra, look for it canned or frozen.

2 tablespoons margarine

8 plum tomatoes, grilled (page 303) and chopped

½ medium onion, sliced, grilled (page 303), and chopped

Puree from 6 cloves Caramelized Garlic (page 302)

1 cup sliced fresh okra

¼ cup chopped scallions

1 teaspoon dried thyme

½ teaspoon Tabasco

Pinch ground nutmeg

*Gather 'Round the Grill*

Preheat the grill or side burner.

**M**elt the margarine in a medium skillet and add the tomatoes, onion, and garlic. Simmer 2 minutes and add the okra, scallions, thyme, Tabasco, and nutmeg. Cook until the okra is tender, about 5 minutes.

# Sweet Potato and Pecan Calzone

### Makes 4 servings

**A** calzone is usually thought of as a pizza dough turnover, stuffed with mozzarella and sausage and deep-fried. My latest version—calzone stuffed with sweet potato and pecans—is grilled and served as a dessert.

If the calzone balloons up while it's baking, prick it with a sharp knife to allow excess steam to escape.

*Grill temperature* **medium**

> **1 cup cooked and mashed sweet potato**
>
> **¼ cup chopped pecans**
>
> **4 tablespoons melted butter**
>
> **¼ cup brown sugar**
>
> **¼ cup granulated sugar**
>
> **2 eggs, lightly beaten**
>
> **2 tablespoons heavy cream**
>
> **1 teaspoon ground cinnamon**
>
> **2 pizza discs (page 304)**
>
> **Confectioners' sugar**

(continued)

*Fall Menu 20*

**P**reheat the grill.

**I**n a medium bowl combine the sweet potato, pecans, 2 tablespoons of the butter, both sugars, eggs, heavy cream, and cinnamon.

**D**ivide the pizza discs in half and roll out each portion on a lightly floured surface into a 6-inch disc.

**P**lace one fourth of the filling on the lower half of each disc and fold down the top halves to make turnovers. Seal the edges by pressing them together with the tines of a fork. Brush tops with the remaining 2 tablespoons butter and place on the grill for 8 to 10 minutes on each side. The calzone is done when the dough sounds hollow when tapped. Sprinkle with confectioners' sugar.

# Menu 21

*Spaghetti with Zucchini and Yellow Squash*

*Shrimp with Tomato Pesto*

*Sweet Potato Cottage Fries*

*Grilled Catfish with Piquant Tomatoes*

*Biscuits and Honey*

**N**ew Orleans is known for its seafood, and entire restaurants are devoted to the treasures of the sea. But what is really unique about New Orleans is jazz. Not only is the city the birthplace of this only example of true American music but it's hard not to hear music coming from open windows as musicians, both good and bad, practice. We should think about, and celebrate, the great sounds of life.

# Spaghetti with Zucchini and Yellow Squash

### Makes 4 servings

**W**hen the grilled zucchini and yellow squash are cut into long narrow strips, they resemble the spaghetti they're mixed with. This is a good way to use up the zucchini from the garden when no one wants to take any more of it off your hands.

**6 to 8 small zucchini, split lengthwise**

**6 to 8 small yellow squash, split lengthwise**

**10 tablespoons olive oil**

**1 pound spaghetti**

**Puree from 1 head Caramelized Garlic (page 302)**

**¼ cup sliced scallions**

**2 tablespoons chopped fresh basil and 8 whole leaves for garnish**

**¼ cup grated Parmesan cheese**

**Freshly ground black pepper to taste**

**P**reheat the grill and side burner.

**B**rush the zucchini and squash with 4 tablespoons of the olive oil and grill over high heat until the vegetables are slightly charred outside. Remove from the grill and cool. Cut the zucchini and squash lengthwise into long narrow ⅛-inch-thick strips resembling spaghetti.

**M**eanwhile, cook the spaghetti until al dente on the side burner or stovetop. Drain well, place in a serving bowl, and toss with 2 tablespoons olive oil. Keep warm while preparing the sauce.

Heat the remaining 4 tablespoons olive oil in a large saucepan on grill or side burner, and sauté the garlic 10 to 15 seconds. Add the zucchini and squash, scallions, and chopped basil, and cook 2 to 3 minutes, tossing occasionally. Combine the sauce with the cooked spaghetti and arrange on a serving platter. Sprinkle with the Parmesan cheese and the black pepper and garnish with the whole basil leaves.

# Shrimp with Tomato Pesto

**Makes 4 servings**

Adding tomato to the basil gives it a sweetness that goes well with the shrimp. Try the dish over pasta. If peeling and deveining shrimp are not your favorite pastime, many fishmongers sell shrimp ready for the pan.

*Grill temperature*
**high**

1½ pounds medium shrimp, peeled and deveined

2 tablespoons olive oil

1 cup chicken stock

½ cup Tomato Pesto (recipe follows)

1 cup heavy cream (optional)

¼ cup grated Parmesan cheese

Freshly ground black pepper to taste

Preheat the grill.

Brush the shrimp with the olive oil and grill over high heat for 5 to 6 minutes, or until almost fully cooked. In a saucepan, heat the stock and the tomato pesto. Add the shrimp, bring to a boil, and add the cream and the cheese and season with black pepper. Remove from the grill and serve with Tomato Pesto.

*Fall*
*Menu 21*

(continued)

# Tomato Pesto

### Makes about 2 cups

**5 plum tomatoes, grilled (page 303), peeled, seeded, and chopped**
**¾ cup fresh basil leaves**
**¼ cup fresh spinach leaves**
**Puree from 1 head Caramelized Garlic (page 302)**
**¼ cup pine nuts or walnuts**
**½ cup grated Parmesan cheese**
**½ cup olive oil**

**P**uree the tomatoes, basil, and spinach in a blender or food processor. Add the garlic, nuts, and cheese and blend well. With the motor going, slowly add the oil.

# Sweet Potato Cottage Fries

### Makes 4 servings

Sweet potatoes are a member of the morning glory family, a tasty way to get lots of vitamins and beta-carotene. Choose medium sweet potatoes with smooth unbruised skins and store them in a dark, dry, and cool spot, not the refrigerator.

Grill temperature
**high-medium**

¼ cup olive oil

Puree from 1 head Caramelized Garlic (page 302)

1 teaspoon ground thyme

1 teaspoon dried rosemary, crumbled

1 teaspoon dried basil

1 teaspoon dried parsley

1 teaspoon dried oregano

¼ teaspoon black pepper

¼ teaspoon cayenne or Tabasco

Pinch ground nutmeg

4 sweet potatoes, baked and cut lengthwise into 4 pieces

Preheat the grill.

In a small bowl combine the olive oil, garlic, thyme, rosemary, basil, parsley, oregano, black pepper, cayenne, and nutmeg and mix well. Place the sweet potatoes in a shallow dish and pour the olive oil mixture over them. Set aside for 15 minutes, turning the potatoes occasionally. Remove from the marinade and place on grill for 4 to 5 minutes, turning once, until slightly charred on the outside.

*Fall Menu 21*

# Grilled Catfish with Piquant Tomatoes

**Makes 4 servings**

*Grill temperature*

——

**high-medium**

**U**p until a few years ago, catfish were found only on the muddy bottoms of rivers, but now they're farm-raised in open pools and are abundant in fish markets. Catfish are fed a balanced and nutritious diet, and are always pure white and sweet-tasting. They've become an economical buy.

**2 teaspoons Tabasco**

**1 teaspoon paprika**

**1 teaspoon ground thyme**

**½ teaspoon ground cumin**

**¼ teaspoon ground nutmeg**

**Salt and pepper to taste**

**2 pounds catfish fillets**

**2 tablespoons olive oil**

**Juice of 1 lemon**

**2 cups Piquant Tomatoes (recipe follows)**

*Gather 'Round the Grill*

**C**ombine the Tabasco, paprika, thyme, cumin, nutmeg, salt, and pepper in a small dish and mix well. Rub the catfish fillets on both sides with the mixture and refrigerate 30 minutes.

**P**reheat the grill.

**B**rush the catfish with the olive oil and lemon juice and grill 3 to 4 minutes on each side. Serve with the Piquant Tomatoes.

# Piquant Tomatoes

### Makes about 2 cups

8 plum tomatoes, split, grilled (page 303), and chopped

2 scallions, chopped

Puree from 2 to 3 cloves Caramelized Garlic (page 302)

3 jalapeño peppers, grilled (page 303), seeded, and coarsely chopped

2 tablespoons red wine vinegar

2 tablespoons olive oil

¼ teaspoon Tabasco

In a medium bowl combine all the ingredients and mix well.


# Biscuits and Honey

### Makes 4 to 6 servings, or 14 to 16 biscuits

Although I had these biscuits served to me for breakfast one morning, I found they also made a very good dessert. Try them with different kinds of honey; the flavor of the honey depends on the blossoms the bees were visiting. Orange blossom honey is light and delicate; raspberry honey has the faint taste and aroma of raspberries. Generally, the darker the honey, the stronger the flavor.

(continued)

*Grill temperature*

**see note**

*Fall
Menu 21*

**201**

3¼ cups all-purpose flour

4 teaspoons baking powder

½ teaspoon salt

½ teaspoon sugar

⅔ cup shortening or margarine, cut into small pieces

1¼ cups milk

4 tablespoons melted butter

¼ cup honey

Whipped cream

Prepare a charcoal or hardwood fire.

In a medium bowl combine the flour, baking powder, salt, and sugar, and toss lightly with a fork. Cut in the shortening or margarine until the mixture resembles coarse crumbs. Slowly add the milk and stir until the mixture comes together. Transfer to a lightly floured surface and knead a few times until the dough is smooth, taking care not to overwork the dough. Roll out to ½ inch thick and place in a well-greased Dutch oven. Cover the pot and place the Dutch oven on the hot coals. Cover the top of the pot with additional coals and bake 15 minutes. Remove the Dutch oven from the coals, uncover, and remove the biscuits.

Cool the biscuits slightly, split in half, and brush with melted butter. Warm them on the grill (do not toast), remove and drizzle them with honey, and top with whipped cream.

NOTE: These biscuits can be baked on a charcoal or gas grill over medium temperature for 7 to 8 minutes with the hood down.

# Menu 22

*Figs in Prosciutto Blankets*

*Rigatoni with Chicken and Black Beans*

*Cabbage Balls*

*Smoked Pork Butt*

*Butt-with-a-Kick Sauce or Butt-with-a-Push Sauce*

*Lemon Meringue Tarts*

The word *barbecue* has been overused and is misunderstood. It's a verb that means to cook food for a long time over a slow fire, and it's the traditional way people have cooked pork and beef in the Deep South for years. *Barbecue* can also mean cooking out-of-doors in a brick fireplace or on a spit. The kind of fast outdoor cooking we do in our backyards over hot coals or an open flame is called grilling, and it's become a ritual to be enjoyed year-round.

# Figs in Prosciutto Blankets

### Makes 4 servings

**E**veryone loves pigs in blankets—tiny frankfurters wrapped in biscuit dough—but have you ever tried this spinoff? Figs in prosciutto blankets, or thin slices of salty prosciutto wrapped around fresh figs?

**8 ripe figs, split in half lengthwise**

**16 thin slices prosciutto**

**2 tablespoons olive oil**

**¼ pound Parmesan or provolone cheese, shaved**

**Freshly ground black pepper**

**P**reheat the grill.

**W**rap each fig half with a slice of prosciutto and secure with a small skewer or toothpick. Lightly brush with olive oil and grill 2 to 3 minutes, turning once. Remove the skewers or toothpicks and top the figs with shaved cheese and a sprinkling of black pepper. Serve immediately.

# Rigatoni with Chicken and Black Beans

**Makes 4 servings**

Rigatoni is a pasta that requires a lot of sauce and this one has South-western undertones that get trapped inside the tubes of pasta.

*Grill temperature*

**high-medium**

**1 pound rigatoni**

**6 tablespoons olive oil**

**1 pound chicken cutlets**

**1 medium onion, thickly sliced, grilled (page 303), and diced**

**Puree from 6 cloves Caramelized Garlic (page 302)**

**One 28-ounce can black beans, rinsed and drained**

**½ cup chopped grilled (page 303) plum tomatoes**

**¼ cup chopped scallions**

**1 teaspoon ground cumin**

**2 cups chicken stock**

**1 tablespoon chopped fresh cilantro**

**½ teaspoon Tabasco**

Cook the rigatoni until al dente. Drain well, place in a bowl, and toss with 2 table-spoons of the olive oil. Keep warm while preparing the chicken.

Preheat the grill.

*(continued)*

*Fall Menu 22*

205

Brush the chicken with 2 tablespoons of the olive oil and grill for 2 to 3 minutes on each side. Remove from grill, cool slightly, and cut into strips.

Heat the remaining 2 tablespoons olive oil in a large saucepan and sauté the onion and garlic for 30 seconds. Add the beans, tomatoes, scallions, and cumin and simmer 2 to 3 minutes. Add the chicken stock, cilantro, and Tabasco and simmer 5 minutes. Add the chicken strips and toss with rigatoni. Serve immediately.

## *Cabbage Balls*

**Makes 4 servings**

*Grill temperature*

**medium, then low-medium**

If you're expecting an army, this traditional Polish stuffed cabbage is a great recipe to make because everyone can help. Line up the ingredients and have one person cook the cabbage, another do the stuffing, and so forth.

1 large head savoy or green cabbage
2 tablespoons olive oil
½ pound spicy bratwurst, chorizo, or Italian sausage, grilled (page 305), cooled, and chopped
1 cup orzo or rice, cooked and drained
1 medium onion, thickly sliced, grilled (page 303), and chopped
1 green bell pepper, grilled (page 302), seeded, and chopped
6 scallions, grilled (page 303) and chopped
Puree from 6 cloves Caramelized Garlic (page 302)
¼ teaspoon ground allspice
½ teaspoon Tabasco
2¼ cups Cabbage Sauce (recipe follows)

Remove 8 of the outer cabbage leaves, discarding any that are damaged. Blanch the outer leaves in very hot water for 2 to 3 minutes or until limp, taking care not to tear them. Cut out and discard the thick center veins. Chop the remaining cabbage.

On the side burner or stovetop, heat the olive oil in a large skillet over medium heat and sauté the chopped cabbage until it is completely cooked. Add the sausage, orzo, onion, bell pepper, scallions, garlic, allspice, and Tabasco and mix well.

Divide the meat mixture into 8 equal portions. Place the blanched leaves, one at a time, on a clean kitchen towel and place some stuffing in the center of each. Fold the cabbage leaves around the stuffing, lift the towel, and shape the ingredients into a ball by twisting the towel tightly around the cabbage.

Place the balls seam side down in an ovenproof dish and pour the sauce over them. Place the dish on the grill at low-medium heat and cook until the cabbage is tender, about 30 minutes, with the grill hood down.

## Cabbage Sauce

**Makes about 1 ¹/₂ cups**

**1 cup tomato sauce**

**¹/₄ cup dry red wine**

**2 tablespoons balsamic vinegar**

**2 tablespoons honey**

**Pinch ground nutmeg**

**Salt and pepper to taste**

Combine all the ingredients in a small saucepan and simmer 2 to 3 minutes. While the sauce is still warm, pour it over the cabbage balls.

# Smoked Pork Butt

**Makes 12 servings**

**E**njoy this smoked pork butt in one of two ways: either with a sauce with a "kick" or another with a "push" (recipes follow). Whichever sauce you choose, the drink of choice should be a cold, crisp amber beer.

> **6- to 8-pound fresh pork butt**
> **½ cup Pork Dry Rub (page 74)**
> **Three 12-ounce bottles strong beer or ale**
> **1 cup sugar**
> **1 medium onion, chopped**
> **2 heads garlic, cloves separated and peeled**
> **2 tablespoons Tabasco**

**R**ub the pork on all sides with the dry rub and refrigerate, loosely covered, for 24 hours.

**P**repare the smoker for 10 hours.

**F**ill the water pan with the beer, sugar, onion, garlic, and Tabasco and stir until the sugar has dissolved. Place the meat in the smoker and smoke at 195° F.

*Gather 'Round the Grill*

**S**oak chunks of hickory in water for 1 hour. After 2 hours of smoking, add the hickory to the smoker.

**W**hen the meat is tender (8 to 9 hours) and pulling away from the bone, remove it from the smoker and let it sit 1 hour before slicing.

# Butt-with-a-Kick Sauce

**Makes about 5 cups**

1 tablespoon olive oil

1 cup finely minced onion

½ cup chopped red bell pepper

4 fresh ancho or serrano chili peppers, grilled (page 303), seeded, and
chopped, or 2 dried chilies

One 10-ounce bottle spicy steak sauce or hot steak sauce

One 12-ounce bottle chili sauce

1 tablespoon Tabasco

1 teaspoon ground cumin

½ cup chopped fresh tomatoes

**H**eat the olive oil in a medium skillet and sweat the onion, bell pepper, and chilies over low heat for a few minutes. Add the steak sauce, chili sauce, Tabasco, and cumin and simmer 4 to 5 minutes. Add the tomatoes and stir well.

*(continued)*

*Fall*
*Menu 22*

# Butt-with-a-Push Sauce

**Makes about 2 1/4 cups**

- 1 cup hoisin sauce
- 1 cup chili sauce
- 1 tablespoon soy sauce
- 1 tablespoon finely chopped scallion (white part only)
- 1 tablespoon red wine vinegar
- 1/2 teaspoon Tabasco

**C**ombine all the ingredients in a medium saucepan and simmer 4 to 5 minutes.

# Lemon Meringue Tarts

## Makes 6 servings

**M**ake sure you use fresh lemon juice for these tarts; frozen or bottled lemon juice is a poor substitute. Many stores sell zesters for removing the rind from citrus peels without getting any of the white pith. Otherwise, peel off strips of the rind with a sharp paring knife and chop fine.

> **2 tablespoons cornstarch**
>
> **4 tablespoons granulated sugar**
>
> **3 egg yolks**
>
> **¼ cup light corn syrup**
>
> **¼ cup fresh lemon juice**
>
> **3 tablespoons butter**
>
> **1 teaspoon lemon zest**
>
> **Six 3-inch prebaked tart shells**
>
> **4 egg whites**
>
> **2 tablespoons confectioners' sugar**

**I**n a small bowl combine the cornstarch and 2 tablespoons of the granulated sugar. Whisk in the egg yolks and set aside.

**I**n a small nonreactive saucepan combine the corn syrup, lemon juice, butter, and lemon zest and heat, stirring constantly, until the mixture comes to a boil. Take the mixture off the heat and slowly add the egg yolk mixture, stirring constantly. Return the pot to the heat and when the mixture comes to a boil, remove and pour the mixture into the tart shells. Set aside to cool.

*(continued)*

**P**reheat the grill.

**B**eat the egg whites until they form soft peaks, add the remaining 2 tablespoons granulated sugar, and continue beating until the egg whites are stiff. Top the tarts with the meringue, sprinkle with confectioners' sugar, place on the top shelf of a grill (or build a shelf with several bricks side-by-side) and brown for 1 minute with the grill hood down.

Winter

# Menu 23

*Boston Brown Bread*

*Split Pea Soup*

*New England Smoked Dinner*

*New England Vegetables*

*Brown Betty*

Food once cooked over an open fire is now cooked on the grill—
a bracing bowl of pea soup, a homey beef brisket, and
an old-fashioned brown betty for dessert. What could be more
appreciated when the wind is blowing and there's the feel of snow
in the air? Time to snuggle up close to the fire and stay warm
and to applaud our country's first settlers, who knew what
cold-weather food was all about.

# Boston Brown Bread

**Makes 2 loaves**

**B**rown bread is an old-fashioned colonial recipe that doesn't require any yeast. The leavening is a combination of baking soda and buttermilk, and the bread is steamed rather than baked in an oven.

> **1 cup yellow cornmeal**
> **1 cup all-purpose flour**
> **1 cup rye flour**
> **¾ cup dry bread crumbs**
> **1 teaspoon baking soda**
> **1 teaspoon salt**
> **2 cups buttermilk**
> **¾ cup molasses**
> **1 cup raisins**

**P**reheat the grill.

**B**utter and flour two 1-pound coffee cans or 4-cup ovenproof containers. In a large bowl combine the cornmeal, flours, bread crumbs, baking soda, and salt and mix well. Add the buttermilk, molasses, and raisins and stir until the dry ingredients are just moistened. Fill the containers two-thirds full, cover securely with aluminum foil, and tie with a string. Place in a Dutch oven and pour in 2 inches of boiling water. Cover and place on the grill. Lower the grill hood and steam the bread for 2 hours, adding more water, if necessary. The bread is done when it pulls slightly away from the sides.

# Split Pea Soup

## Makes 6 to 8 servings

Split pea soup was invented to use up ham bones. It's the favorite hearty meal for a wintry night and is traditionally served with flavored croutons. For an up-to-date treat, try grilled sourdough-bread croutons. If you like your soup creamy, puree it in a blender or food processor once the split peas are tender.

*Grill temperature*

**medium, then low**

2 cups split peas

2 tablespoons butter

1 medium onion, thickly sliced, grilled (page 303), and diced

½ cup diced celery

½ cup peeled and diced carrot

8 cups chicken or vegetable stock

½ cup peeled and diced parsnip

½ cup peeled and diced potato

1 cup diced grilled (page 305) ham

1 ham bone

2 bay leaves

¼ teaspoon Tabasco

Salt and pepper to taste

Place the split peas in a large bowl, cover with 8 cups water, and soak for 24 hours. Drain peas and discard water.

Preheat the grill or side burner.

*(continued)*

*Winter Menu 23*

**H**eat the butter in a 4-quart pot on the grill or side burner over medium heat. Add the onion, celery, and carrot and cook until the vegetables are golden, 2 to 3 minutes. Add the stock, soaked split peas, parsnip, potato, ham, ham bone, bay leaves, and Tabasco. Bring to a boil, lower heat, and simmer 1 hour or until the peas are tender. Remove any bits of ham from the bone and add them to the soup. Discard the bay leaves and ham bone. Season with salt and pepper.

# New England Smoked Dinner

**Makes 8 to 10 servings**

Grill
Temerature
**indirect
cooking**

T he extra fat on a brisket will keep it moist and juicy during the long, low heat smoking process, so don't trim the meat. The fat tends to continuously baste the meat and keep it tender.

If your family turns up their noses at boiled vegetables, especially the root ones, place the boiled vegetables in the smoker for ten minutes and they'll pick up a smoky flavor.

> **6- to 8-pound fresh beef brisket**
>
> **2 tablespoons Tabasco**
>
> **1 cup Beef Smoke Rub (recipe follows)**
>
> **New England Beef Smoker Water (page 221)**
>
> **Boiled vegetables such as parsnips, rutabagas, turnips, cabbage, potatoes, onions, carrots**

**R**ub the brisket with the Tabasco and the smoke rub and place in the refrigerator for a minimum of 2 days.

**P**repare the smoker for up to 10 hours. Hickory chunks may be used, but fruit woods are softer and work best for this recipe. (If you're using your grill as a smoker, the meat will take 6 hours to cook. In a smoker, it will take 8 to 9 hours at 195° F. to become fork-tender.

**F**ill the smoker pan with New England Beef Smoker Water and slowly smoke the meat. When the meat is cooked, let it rest 1 hour, then trim off the excess fat before slicing. Serve with an assortment of boiled vegetables.

*(continued)*

Winter
Menu 23

**219**

# Beef Smoke Rub

**Makes about 1 1/4 cups**

1/4 cup dried parsley

1/4 cup sugar

1/4 cup sweet paprika

8 to 10 bay leaves, crushed

4 cloves garlic, pressed

1 tablespoon garlic powder

1 tablespoon dried thyme

1 tablespoon crushed black peppercorns

1 tablespoon mustard seeds

1 teaspoon ground allspice

1/2 teaspoon ground nutmeg

Combine all the ingredients in a small bowl and mix well.

# New England Beef Smoker Water

**Makes 14 cups**

2 quarts hot water

1 quart cider vinegar

2 cups molasses

6 to 8 bay leaves

4 whole cloves

Vegetable trimmings such as potato skins, carrot peelings,
onion skins, celery leaves

Fill the smoker water tray with the ingredients.

# Brown Betty

**Makes 5 to 6 servings**

*Grill temperature*

**medium**

**B**rown Betty is an old New England dessert made from staples that would last through the winter. This country's first settlers satisfied their sweet tooth by combining bread, whatever fat they had, some stored apples, spices, and sugar and baking the mixture to make a tasty confection.

> **2 cups fresh bread crumbs**
> **¼ cup melted margarine**
> **4 cups sliced apples, grilled (page 305)**
> **¼ cup brown sugar**
> **Juice of 1 lemon**
> **¼ teaspoon ground cinnamon**
> **Pinch ground nutmeg**
> **1 cup hot water**

**P**reheat the grill.

**C**ombine the bread crumbs and the margarine in a medium bowl and mix with a fork until crumbs form. Cover the bottom of a buttered 9-inch baking pan with half the crumb mixture.

*Gather 'Round the Grill*

**I**n a medium bowl combine the apples, brown sugar, lemon juice, cinnamon, and nutmeg and mix well. Top the crumb mixture with half the apples. Repeat with a layer of crumbs (save a few for the top layer) and a layer of apples. Top with the reserved crumbs. Pour the water over the mixture, cover with foil, and bake on grill for 15 minutes with the hood down. Remove the foil and bake, uncovered, 10 additional minutes.

# Menu 24

*Hickory Spit-Roasted Chicken*

*Mushroom Pie*

*Green Bean Gratin*

*Barbecued Veal Shanks*

*Grilled Pears with Raspberry Sauce*

While building that award-winning snowman in your backyard, you want to cook food that doesn't require too much time standing guard over the grill. Or if you're out on the slopes where you hear nothing except the crunch of snow, it would be nice to come home and share a meal with friends gathered around a roaring fire.

# Hickory Spit-Roasted Chicken

**Makes 12 servings**

*Grill temperature*

**medium-low**

These chickens are easy to cook and are ideal for a party or to have on hand over a holiday weekend, when unexpected company may drop in. Serve warm slices of chicken over salad greens, mix chilled chunks with dressing for a chicken salad, or spread slices with a spicy mustard for a sandwich filling.

> **Three 3-pound chickens**
> **1 cup Hickory Chicken Rub (recipe follows)**
> **¼ cup olive oil**
> **1 cup hickory wood chips, soaked 30 minutes in water**

Preheat the grill.

Place the hickory chips into an iron smoker box and put on the grill for the last 20 minutes of cooking.

Rub the chickens on all sides with the rub. Tie the drumsticks together with cord and tuck the wings behind the back. Insert the spit rod through the cavity of the chicken and secure with adjustable holding forks, taking care the chicken is balanced on the rod. Cook the chicken on the rotisserie for about 45 minutes with the cover down or until juices run clear, basting several times with the olive oil. The chicken can also be cooked for 1½ hours on an open spit.

# Hickory Chicken Rub

**Makes about 1 cup**

¼ cup sweet paprika

¼ cup potato starch or flour

1 tablespoon dried thyme

1 tablespoon garlic powder

1 tablespoon lemon pepper, or ½ tablespoon black pepper and
   ½ tablespoon grated lemon rind

1 tablespoon dried rosemary

1 teaspoon ground nutmeg

1 teaspoon ground allspice

**C**ombine all ingredients in a small bowl and mix well.

Winter
Menu 24

# Mushroom Pie

### Makes 6 to 8 servings

**W**edges of mushroom pie can be served as an appetizer or as a side dish with grilled steak. The crust is prepared from thin slices of French bread, which makes it a little unusual.

> **12 very thin slices French bread**
>
> **¼ cup olive oil**
>
> **2 cups grilled (page 303) and chopped, fresh mushrooms (white, cremini, shiitake)**
>
> **1 medium potato, peeled, boiled, and chopped**
>
> **2 red, green, or yellow bell peppers, grilled (page 302), seeded, and chopped**
>
> **1 medium onion, thickly sliced, grilled (page 303), and chopped**
>
> **Puree from 1 head Caramelized Garlic (page 302)**
>
> **1 egg, slightly beaten**
>
> **2 tablespoons milk or cream**
>
> **1 tablespoon dried parsley**
>
> **1 teaspoon Tabasco**
>
> **Pinch ground nutmeg**

**P**reheat the grill.

**P**ress the French bread slices firmly into a buttered 9-inch pie plate and brush with olive oil.

**I**n a separate bowl combine the mushrooms, potato, bell pepper, onion, and garlic and mix well. Add the egg, milk, parsley, Tabasco, and nutmeg and mix again. Place the mixture into the pie plate and bake on grill for 12 to 15 minutes with the grill hood down.

# Green Bean Gratin

**Makes 4 to 6 servings**

When we were growing up, my sister and I hated green beans. As soon as our mother's back was turned, we would toss the beans into each other's dish. Finally, in desperation, she came up with a gratin presentation for the beans and they went down a lot easier.

*Grill temperature*

**high**

> **2 tablespoons margarine**
> **1½ pounds green beans**
> **Puree from 6 to 8 cloves Caramelized Garlic (page 302)**
> **¼ cup dry bread crumbs**
> **1 tablespoon chopped fresh mint**
> **1 tablespoon grated Parmesan cheese**
> **Freshly ground black pepper to taste**

On the stovetop, cook the beans in lightly salted water until almost tender, 8 to 10 minutes.

Preheat the grill or side burner.

Melt the margarine in gratin pan and add the garlic and beans and toss together. Add the bread crumbs, mint, cheese, and pepper. Cook, stirring frequently, for 4 to 5 minutes or until crumbs brown lightly.

*Winter Menu 24*

# Barbecued Veal Shanks

## Makes 4 servings

*Grill temperature*

**high, then medium**

**A**lthough this recipe calls for veal shanks, you can substitute lamb shanks. Add extra flavor to the sweet-and-sour barbecue sauce by tossing in a few grilled mushrooms and bell peppers about a half hour before the shanks are tender.

> **4 pounds veal shanks**
>
> **2 tablespoons olive oil**
>
> **1 medium onion, thickly sliced, grilled (page 303), and chopped**
>
> **4 plum tomatoes, split, grilled (page 303), and chopped**
>
> **1 cup chicken stock**
>
> **1 cup tomato puree**
>
> **½ cup cider vinegar**
>
> **½ cup dark brown sugar**
>
> **Puree from 1 head Caramelized Garlic (page 302)**
>
> **2 tablespoons balsamic vinegar**
>
> **2 bay leaves**
>
> **½ teaspoon Tabasco**

*Gather 'Round the Grill*

**H**ave the butcher cut the shanks crosswise into 1½- to 2-inch pieces.

**B**rush the veal on all sides with olive oil and sear on all sides on a hot grill until they're nicely brown.

In a large saucepan on the grill, combine the onion, plum tomatoes, chicken stock, tomato puree, cider vinegar, brown sugar, garlic, balsamic vinegar, bay leaves, and Tabasco and stir well. Add the veal pieces, bring to a boil, lower heat, cover, and simmer until the meat can be easily pierced with a fork and begins to fall away from the bone, about 1½ to 2 hours. Discard bay leaves.

# Grilled Pears with Raspberry Sauce

**Makes 4 servings**

*Grill temperature*

**medium**

**I**f you like, substitute blackberries or blueberries for the raspberries with their corresponding preserves. Fresh or frozen berries can be used, but taste them first; if they're tart, add a little sugar.

> **4 ripe Bosc or Anjou pears**
> **2 tablespoons melted margarine**
> **1 cup fresh or frozen raspberries**
> **1 cup seedless raspberry preserves**
> **2 tablespoons orange juice**

**P**reheat the grill.

**P**eel the pears, cut in half, and remove the cores. Brush the pear halves with the margarine and grill until they show char marks, 4 to 5 minutes.

**I**n a small saucepan simmer three-fourths of the raspberries, the preserves, and orange juice for 4 to 5 minutes. Press the sauce through a strainer, discarding the seeds.

**P**our the sauce evenly onto 4 dessert dishes, topping each with one of the pear halves, cut side down. Garnish with the remaining raspberries.

# Menu 25

*Grilled Stuffed Clams*

*German Potato Soup*

*Beans with Smoked Ham*

*Long Island Duck with Sauerkraut*

*Apple Dumplings*

Cold-weather sports call for cold-weather foods. While many summertime grillers would never consider grilling during the winter months, once you've tried it, you'll never store away that grill when the weather dips below 50 degrees. Make sure you're in warm clothing, including a hat with ear muffs. When this hearty food gets to the table, no one will care if the wind is blowing or if the hockey team won. All they'll think about is what a good friend you are.

# Grilled Stuffed Clams

## Makes 4 servings

*Grill temperature*

**medium-high**

Everyone has a favorite recipe for stuffed clams and this one is mine. Enjoy them while you're waiting for the other dishes to finish cooking on the grill.

**1 cup dry bread crumbs**

**⅓ cup olive oil**

**¼ cup chopped grilled (page 303) onion**

**Puree from 6 cloves Caramelized Garlic (page 302)**

**1 tablespoon grated Parmesan cheese**

**1 teaspoon chopped fresh Italian parsley**

**1 teaspoon Tabasco**

**16 littleneck clams, well scrubbed and on the half-shell**

**Lemon wedges or Garlic Mayonnaise Dip (page 51)**

Preheat the grill.

In a medium bowl combine the bread crumbs, olive oil, onion, garlic, cheese, parsley, and Tabasco and mix well. Top each of the clams with 2 tablespoons of stuffing and pack it down tightly. Place the clams on grill for 2 minutes, then move to the top shelf (or place 2 bricks in the center of the grate) and lower the grill cover for 5 to 7 minutes. Serve with lemon wedges or garlic dip.

# German Potato Soup

**Makes 6 to 8 servings**

On a cold morning, get up very early and make yourself a pot of this soup, then go out and shovel the driveway or have a day on the slopes; when you get back, you'll have a hearty, warm dish to enjoy. Or if it's a warm morning, still get up very early, make the soup, and let it chill. You'll have a refreshing potato soup when you come back from the beach.

2 tablespoons butter

1 cup diced grilled (page 303) onion

½ cup diced grilled (page 303) scallions

3 cloves garlic, chopped

2 tablespoons all-purpose flour

2 tablespoons sugar

2 tablespoons cider vinegar

6 cups chicken stock

3 cups peeled and diced potatoes

¼ cup chopped fresh chives

2 bay leaves

¼ teaspoon Tabasco

Pinch ground nutmeg

2 cups half-and-half or heavy cream

*(continued)*

*Grill temperature*

**medium, then low**

*Winter Menu 25*

**P**reheat the grill or side burner.

**H**eat the butter in a 4-quart pot on the grill. Add the onion, scallions, and garlic, and cook over medium heat 2 to 3 minutes, taking care not to color the vegetables. Stir in the flour and cook for 2 minutes. Stir in the sugar and vinegar and then the chicken stock, potatoes, chives, bay leaves, Tabasco, and nutmeg. Bring the soup to a boil, lower heat, and simmer 45 minutes. Stir in the half-and-half or heavy cream and reheat to serving temperature. Discard bay leaves.

# Beans with Smoked Ham

### Makes 4 servings

Grill temperature

**medium-low**

Beans, by themselves, are pretty bland, so anything added to the pot to flavor them can only help; besides, this is a good way to use up Sunday's ham bone. This recipe is best prepared in a Dutch oven.

**1 pound white beans such as pea, navy, or cannellini, soaked in 2 quarts water overnight and drained**

**1 smoked ham bone or 2 smoked ham hocks**

**1 medium onion, thickly sliced, grilled (page 303), and chopped**

**1 carrot, peeled and diced**

**Puree from 4 cloves Caramelized Garlic (page 302)**

**2 cups Grilled Tomato Sauce (page 290)**

**1 cup chicken stock**

**1 teaspoon Tabasco**

**2 bay leaves**

**½ teaspoon ground allspice**

Preheat the grill or side burner.

Place the ham bone or ham hocks in a large, heavy pot on the grill or side burner and slowly melt off any fat. Add the onion, carrot, and garlic and simmer 2 to 3 minutes. Add the tomato sauce, stock, drained beans, Tabasco, bay leaves, and allspice. Bring to a boil over medium heat, lower heat, cover, and simmer until the beans are tender, about 1 hour, adding additional water or stock if the beans are dry. Uncover, pick off the meat from the bones, and return it to the pot; discard bones and the bay leaves.

Winter Menu 25

# Long Island Duck with Sauerkraut

### Makes 4 servings

Grill
temperature
**medium**

**M**ost people think that duck is eaten only with fruit or a highly sweet sauce. Try serving duck with something on the sour side, such as sauerkraut.

6 cloves garlic, sliced

1 teaspoon dried rosemary, crumbled

1 teaspoon dried thyme

¼ teaspoon freshly ground black pepper

Two 4½-pound fresh Long Island ducks, split in half

Apples and Kraut (recipe follows)

**I**n a small bowl combine the garlic, rosemary, thyme, and black pepper and mix well.

**P**lace the ducks on a flat surface, skin side up. Gently lift the skin up and place the seasoning mix between the skin and the flesh. Wrap each half in aluminum foil.

**P**reheat the grill.

**C**ook the ducks 45 to 50 minutes with the grill hood down. Remove the ducks from the foil, place in a large pan over the Apples and Kraut, and cook 25 to 30 minutes longer. Remove the ducks from the pan and place on the grill over direct heat for 2 to 3 minutes to crisp up. Serve with the Apples and Kraut.

Gather
'Round
the
Grill

# Apples and Kraut

**Makes 4 servings**

*Grill
temperature*
___
**low**

**4 strips bacon, coarsely chopped**

**1 small onion, sliced**

**2 Granny Smith or other green apples**

**½ cup chicken stock**

**¼ cup dry white wine**

**2 tablespoons cider vinegar**

**2 tablespoons light brown sugar**

**1 teaspoon caraway seeds**

**1 potato, peeled and finely grated**

**4 cups fresh sauerkraut, rinsed and drained well**

**H**eat the bacon, onion, and apple in a nonstick skillet on the grill until the bacon begins to crisp. Drain off any fat, add the remaining ingredients, and mix well. Cover and cook for 20 minutes, or until potato is tender.

# Apple Dumplings

### Makes 4 servings

**W**hen I was very young, I couldn't understand how they got the whole cooked apple inside the pastry. I guess it was no wonder that when I started to bake, this was one of the first things I attempted.

> **4 baking apples, cored and peeled**
>
> **Four 6 x 6-inch sheets pie crust or prepared flaky pastry dough**
>
> **2 tablespoons granulated sugar**
>
> **2 tablespoons chopped nuts (walnuts, pecans)**
>
> **1 teaspoon ground cinnamon**
>
> **4 tablespoons melted butter**
>
> **Confectioners' sugar**

**P**reheat the grill.

**P**lace the apples in the center of the pastry squares. Fill the centers evenly with the sugar, nuts, and cinnamon. Fold the pastry over the apples and brush all sides with the melted butter. Arrange the dumplings in a buttered pan and place on a raised shelf. Lower the grill hood and bake for 25 minutes. Cool slightly and sprinkle with confectioners' sugar.

# Menu 26

*Sausage Gumbo*

*Grilled Soft-Shell Crabs with Chive Dressing*

*Jambalaya*

*Praline Bananas*

As delicious as it may be, traditional Creole-Cajun food is known for its use of butter, cream, and fried foods. Today's lifestyle demands high flavor but with lower calories, so although these recipes are not "diet food," we haven't sacrificed taste although we've cut down on the fat. There is no roux in the gumbo, the soft-shell crabs are not fried, and the dessert has only 2 tablespoons of butter. Celebrate losing those five extra pounds by buying that new suit or dress.

# Sausage Gumbo

**Makes 6 to 8 servings**

*Grill temperature*

**low, then medium, then low**

**O**ne night after filming a segment of our first series, there was some food left over. We put it all together and came up with this version of a sausage gumbo. True, the dish doesn't begin with a classic roux of flour and oil, but it does have the "holy trinity" of onions, peppers, and celery.

¼ **pound bacon or fatback, finely chopped**

½ **cup finely chopped grilled onion (page 303)**

½ **cup seeded and diced grilled green bell pepper (page 302)**

½ **cup diced celery**

**Puree from 8 to 10 cloves Caramelized Garlic (page 302)**

**8 cups chicken stock**

½ **cup diced grilled scallions (page 303)**

½ **pound smoked ham, grilled (page 305) and diced**

½ **teaspoon Tabasco**

**1 bay leaf**

**1 pound spicy smoked sausage or andouille, grilled (page 305) and cut into ½-inch slices**

**2 cups sliced fresh or frozen okra**

1½ **tablespoons gumbo file dissolved in 2 tablespoons water**

**Hot cooked white rice**

*Gather 'Round the Grill*

**P**reheat the grill or side burner.

In a 4-quart pot combine the bacon and onion and simmer over low heat until the bacon is light brown, taking care not to burn it. Raise the heat and add the green pepper, celery, and garlic and simmer 2 minutes. Add the stock, scallions, ham, Tabasco, and bay leaf. Reduce heat and simmer 30 minutes. Add the sausage and okra to the gumbo and simmer 5 to 10 minutes, or until the okra is cooked. Stir in the gumbo file mixture and cook 2 to 3 minutes longer. Discard the bay leaf. Serve over hot cooked white rice.

*Winter*
*Menu 26*

# Grilled Soft-Shell Crabs with Chive Dressing

**Makes 4 servings**

*Grill temperature*

**high-medium**

**A**crab is called a soft-shell from the time it casts off its old shell until the new one has time to harden. Serve these crabs with Chive Dressing, lettuce, sliced tomatoes, and lots of crusty bread.

**8 soft-shell crabs, fresh or frozen, cleaned**

### For the Marinade

**½ cup milk**

**Puree from 2 or 3 cloves Caramelized Garlic (page 302)**

**¼ teaspoon ground nutmeg**

**¼ teaspoon Tabasco**

### For Basting Sauce

**¼ cup olive oil**

**Juice of 2 lemons**

**1 tablespoon chopped fresh Italian parsley**

**1 teaspoon Tabasco**

**¼ teaspoon ground paprika**

**2 cups Chive Dressing (recipe follows)**

*Gather 'Round the Grill*

**H**ave your fishmonger clean the crabs.

In a shallow dish combine the milk, garlic, nutmeg, and Tabasco and mix well. Marinate the crabs in this mixture for 1 hour in the refrigerator.

Preheat the grill.

In a small bowl combine the olive oil, lemon juice, parsley, Tabasco, and paprika and mix well. Place the crabs on the grill and brush with the basting mixture several times while they're cooking. Grill 4 minutes, turn the crabs over, and cook another 3 to 4 minutes. The total cooking time should be 7 to 8 minutes. Serve with Chive Dressing.

## Chive Dressing

**Makes about 2¼ cups**

1 cup mayonnaise, regular or low-fat

1 cup sour cream, regular or low-fat

¼ cup finely chopped chives

Juice of 1 lemon

Puree from 3 cloves Caramelized Garlic (page 302)

2 tablespoons chopped fresh Italian parsley

¼ teaspoon Tabasco

Salt and pepper to taste

In a medium bowl combine all the ingredients and mix well.

# Jambalaya

### Makes 6 servings

**L**ouisiana Cajuns differ on the proper consistency of the rice in a jambalaya. If you prefer your jambalaya to have a drier consistency, uncover the pot for the last 5 minutes. If you like it with more liquid, add a little more stock at the end. You can add some grilled shrimp, if you like, or a few shucked oysters about 5 minutes before the stew is ready. To really make the flavors stand out, add some smoked fish.

**2 pounds boneless pork chops, grilled 4 to 6 minutes on each side and coarsely chopped**

**1 pound ham steak, ¼ inch thick, grilled (page 305) and coarsely chopped**

**1 pound smoked pork sausage, grilled (page 305) and sliced**

**½ pound bacon or fatback, cut into small pieces**

**2 medium onions, thickly sliced, grilled (page 303) and diced**

**2 red and 2 green bell peppers, grilled (page 302), seeded, and diced**

**3 ribs celery, sliced**

**6 scallions, grilled (page 303) and diced**

**Puree from 1 head Caramelized Garlic (page 302)**

**3 bay leaves**

**1½ teaspoons dried parsley**

**1½ teaspoons dried basil**

**1½ teaspoons dried thyme**

**1 teaspoon sweet or hot paprika**

**1 teaspoon dried coriander**

1 teaspoon Tabasco

4 plum tomatoes, split, grilled (page 303), and chopped

1 cup tomato puree

2 cups chicken stock

1 cup long-grain rice

1 cup sliced fresh or frozen okra

Preheat the grill and side burner.

Place the pork chops, ham, sausage, and bacon in a large, heavy stockpot and, stirring constantly, cook over high heat for 5 minutes.

Add the onions, bell peppers, celery, scallions, garlic, bay leaves, parsley, basil, thyme, paprika, coriander, and Tabasco. Lower the heat to medium and cook 5 minutes, stirring constantly.

Add the plum tomatoes and puree and cook 2 to 3 minutes. Stir in the stock and bring to a boil. Add the rice and okra, lower the heat, cover, and simmer 15 to 20 minutes.

# Praline Bananas

**Makes 4 servings**

*Grill temperature*

**medium**

**P**ralines are patty-shaped candies from New Orleans, made from pecans and brown sugar. And bananas combined with praline sauce make a very special ending to a Creole-style dinner.

> 1 cup brown sugar
> 2 tablespoons butter
> ¼ cup chopped pecans
> ¼ cup cream
> 4 ripe bananas, peeled and cut into ½-inch slices

**P**reheat the grill.

**I**n a medium saucepan heat the brown sugar until it melts and, stirring constantly, cook for 30 seconds. Stir in the butter and simmer 1 minute. Add the pecans and cook 1 minute. Stir in the cream and simmer 30 to 45 seconds. Add the bananas and toss gently. Serve warm.

# Menu 27
## Easter

*Sunday Pasta*

*Eggplant and Olives*

*Grilled Fennel*

*Breast of Veal*

*Holiday Stuffing*

*Melon and Wine*

Until the twelfth century, the New Year began appropriately in March, when the first green leaves appear. It's the time of year to shake off the old and put on the new. If you've stored your grill for the winter, drag it out and start cooking outdoors again. Spring always means rebirth and coincides with the celebration of renewed life, which, for Christians, means Easter.

# Sunday Pasta

**Makes 8 servings**

*Grill Temperature*

**high, then low**

**T**his isn't a recipe you prepare when you come home after a long day at work. This pasta sauce is unique, and you want to save it for a special occasion, when you have the time not only to cook but to spend time savoring all the wonderful flavors. Serve the sauce over penne, or any other short tube pasta with holes that can hold the sauce.

2½- to 3-pound beef top round (London broil)
½ cup olive oil
4 cups Grilled Tomato Sauce (page 290) or your favorite tomato sauce
2 large onions, thickly sliced, grilled (page 303), and chopped
1 cup dry red wine
¼ pound smoked ham steak, ¼ inch thick, grilled (page 305) and diced
1 or 2 chicken livers, rinsed, trimmed, and grilled (page 305)
3 or 4 fresh white mushrooms, grilled (page 303) and sliced
1 small eggplant, sliced, grilled (page 303), and diced
2 pounds penne
¼ cup grated Parmesan cheese

*Gather 'Round the Grill*

**P**reheat the grill.

**B**rush the beef on all sides with the olive oil and grill over high heat for 4 minutes on each side.

**I**n a large saucepan combine the tomato sauce, onions, and wine. Add the grilled beef and simmer over low heat until the meat is very tender, 1½ to 2 hours.

**J**ust before serving, add the grilled ham, chicken liver, mushrooms, and eggplant to the sauce and stir well.

**C**ook the penne until al dente.

**R**emove the beef from the sauce, shred it into thin strips, and toss with the pasta. Place the pasta on a serving platter, top with the sauce, and sprinkle with cheese.

# Eggplant and Olives

**Makes 4 servings**

**E**ggplant is like a sponge and absorbs whatever flavors it comes into contact with. In this case it's tomatoes, garlic, and black olives. Serve as a side dish or as a topping for bruschetta—toasted slices of Tuscan bread.

> 2 small eggplants, cut into finger-size pieces
> 6 ripe plum tomatoes, split
> 4 tablespoons olive oil
> ¼ cup cured black olives, pitted and chopped
> Puree from 1 head Caramelized Garlic (page 302)
> 8 to 10 fresh basil leaves, chopped
> Freshly ground black pepper

**P**reheat the grill.

**B**rush the eggplant and tomatoes with 2 tablespoons of the olive oil and place on grill for 4 to 5 minutes, turning once. Remove the vegetables and place in a medium bowl with the remaining 2 tablespoons olive oil, olives, garlic, and basil. Toss gently and sprinkle with black pepper.

*Grill temperature*

**high-medium**

*Holidays Menu 27*

# Grilled Fennel

**Makes 4 servings**

ennel has a white bulbous base with layers that peel off like celery ribs and a top of green feathery fronds. It is best known in the Mediterranean countries, though lately it has been cultivated in California. It can be eaten raw, braised, grilled, and sautéed and has a slight anise or licorice flavor.

> **2 medium fennel bulbs**
> **¼ cup flavored olive oil**
> **Freshly ground black pepper**

**C**ut off and discard the fennel stems, and trim off any brown spots. Cut the bulb into quarters through the core.

**P**reheat the grill.

**B**rush the fennel with the olive oil and place on the outer edge of the grill, not directly over the heat. Brushing occasionally with the oil, cook the fennel for 20 minutes. Move the fennel to high heat for 30 to 60 seconds to crisp it just before serving. Sprinkle with black pepper.

# Breast of Veal

## Makes 6 servings

Once the breast of veal is stuffed, secure it with skewers or toothpicks. It's a good idea to count the toothpicks you use and remove the same number before you serve the roast so that your guests don't have any surprises.

It's traditional good luck to set three shelled hard-cooked eggs end to end in the stuffing. When the roast is carved, the egg slices give the stuffing a nice presentation.

*Grill temperature*

**high, then low**

Holiday Stuffing (recipe follows), chilled

4- to 5-pound breast of veal with a pocket cut in

¼ cup olive oil

2 cups chicken stock

2 cups tomato sauce

1 cup red wine

Salt and pepper to taste

Preheat the grill.

Stuff the dressing into the pocket of the veal breast. Secure the ends with skewers or toothpicks. Brush the oil onto all sides of the veal.

Place the veal on the grill and sear over high heat on all sides. Transfer the meat to an ovenproof pan and add the chicken stock, tomato sauce, and wine. Bring to a boil, lower heat, cover the pan, and lower the grill hood. Simmer until the veal is tender, about 1½ hours. After the roast has rested for 15 to 20 minutes, cut it into slices between the ribs.

*Holidays Menu 27*

(continued)

# Holiday Stuffing

**Makes about 8 cups**

1 pound spicy sausage, grilled (page 305), cooled, and removed
   from casing

3 cups crumbled day-old bread

1 medium onion, thickly sliced, grilled (page 303), and chopped

½ cup chopped celery

¾ cup chicken or beef stock

One 8-ounce jar applesauce

1 egg, lightly beaten

1 teaspoon poultry seasoning

1 teaspoon dried basil

1 teaspoon dried parsley

½ teaspoon Tabasco

**I**n a large bowl combine the sausage, bread, onion, celery, and stock and mix well. Add the applesauce, egg, poultry seasoning, basil, parsley, and Tabasco and blend well. Chill mixture until ready to use.

# Melon and Wine

### Makes 4 servings

A dry red wine like Chianti is a good choice because of the sweetness of the melon. If you make this in advance and chill it in the refrigerator, the flavors will only get better.

*Grill temperature*

**high**

**1 large ripe honeydew or casaba melon, peeled and seeded**

**3 tablespoons light corn syrup**

**1 tablespoon melted butter or margarine**

**1 teaspoon chopped fresh mint**

**2 to 3 cups dry red wine**

Preheat the grill.

Cut the melon into finger-size pieces. In a large bowl combine the corn syrup, butter, and mint and marinate the melon for 10 to 15 minutes. Remove the melon and sear on a hot grill. Cool and place in stemmed wine glasses. Cover the melon with the wine and let sit 30 minutes before serving.

*Holidays Menu 27*

# Menu 28
## Mother's Day

*Grilled Tomato—Basil Soup*

*Asparagus Bundles*

*Grilled Coho Salmon Fillets with Couscous Salad*

*Fruit Parcels*

On the second Sunday in May, children pay tribute to their mothers (and grandmothers). The day was conceived in 1907 by Anna Jarvis of Philadelphia, in honor of her mother. Originally the day was marked with a special church service to which the congregation wore pink or white carnations, but the holiday has grown from sending cards to giving presents to inviting Mom out for dinner so she doesn't have to cook. Mother-in-law's Day, launched on March 5, 1934, by the editor of a paper in Amarillo, Texas, somehow never caught on. Mom will have a hard time finding fault with any of her brood when she's invited to share a menu like this one.

# Grilled Tomato—Basil Soup

**Makes 8 to 10 servings**

Grill
temperature

**medium,
then low**

**T**he combination of tomatoes and basil is hard to improve upon. Most often the two are blended together in a salad, but here they're mixed together in a soup. Depending on your calorie allotment, use half-and-half or heavy cream.

**4 to 5 large ripe tomatoes, grilled (page 303) and chopped**

**2 medium onions, thickly sliced, grilled (page 303), and chopped**

**Puree from 1 head Caramelized Garlic (page 302)**

**½ cup chopped fresh basil**

**2 tablespoons butter**

**2 tablespoons all-purpose flour**

**1 cup tomato puree**

**4 cups chicken stock**

**2 bay leaves**

**1 teaspoon dried thyme**

**½ teaspoon ground allspice**

**½ teaspoon Tabasco**

**Salt and pepper to taste**

**1 cup half-and-half or heavy cream**

Gather
'Round
the
Grill

**P**reheat the grill or side burner.

Combine the tomatoes, onion, and garlic in a 4-quart pot and simmer 4 to 5 minutes over medium heat. Add the basil and the butter and cook until the butter melts. Add the flour and cook 2 to 3 minutes. Stir in the tomato puree and cook 2 to 3 minutes longer. Add the chicken stock, bay leaves, thyme, allspice, Tabasco, salt, and pepper and simmer 30 to 35 minutes. Remove the soup from the heat, pour into a food mill, and puree. Return the soup to the pot, bring to a boil, and add the half-and-half or cream. Lower heat and simmer 2 minutes.

# Asparagus Bundles

### Makes 4 to 6 servings

*Grill temperature*

**medium**

**W**rapping these asparagus in prosciutto contributes to their appearance and sets the vegetable off as something special. By peeling off the tough skin at the end of the asparagus, you get to eat more of it.

> **32 pencil-thin asparagus**
> **10 to 12 thin slices prosciutto or Black Forest–style smoked ham**
> **½ cup olive oil**
> **Juice of 1 lemon**
> **1 tablespoon grated Parmesan cheese**
> **1 teaspoon chopped fresh basil**
> **Freshly ground black pepper**
> **1 cup Garlic Mayonnaise Dip (page 51)**

**P**eel the ends of the asparagus with a vegetable peeler and then blanch the asparagus 4 to 5 minutes in boiling water. Drain, pat dry, and wrap 3 to 4 asparagus stalks in each prosciutto slice. Wrap each bundle with butcher's twine or secure with a toothpick. Combine the olive oil, lemon juice, Parmesan cheese, and basil in a shallow dish and marinate the bundles in this mixture for 30 minutes.

**P**reheat the grill.

**R**emove the asparagus bundles from the marinade and grill until slightly charred, 3 to 5 minutes. Sprinkle with black pepper and serve with Garlic Mayonnaise Dip.

*Gather 'Round the Grill*

# Grilled Coho Salmon Fillets with Couscous Salad

Makes 4 servings

**F**irm-textured coho salmon has pink to reddish-orange flesh and tastes faintly like trout. All kinds of salmon are high in vitamin A and many of the B vitamins as well as omega-3 oils. Salmon is an American fish found in both the Atlantic and Pacific oceans.

*Grill temperature*

**high for salmon; medium for sauce**

> **Four 8-ounce coho salmon fillets**
>
> **2 tablespoons olive oil**
>
> **Juice of 1 lemon**
>
> **1 tablespoon finely chopped fresh mint**
>
> **¼ cup light corn syrup**
>
> **Juice of 1 orange**
>
> **1 tablespoon red wine vinegar**
>
> **¼ teaspoon Tabasco**
>
> **Couscous Salad (recipe follows)**

**P**reheat the grill.

**B**rush the fillets with a mixture of the oil, lemon juice, and mint. Place on a very hot grill and cook 2 to 3 minutes on each side. Remove and chill 30 minutes.

**I**n a small saucepan combine the corn syrup, orange juice, vinegar, and Tabasco and simmer 3 to 4 minutes over medium heat. Cool and brush over the salmon just before serving.

*Holidays Menu 28*

*(continued)*

# Couscous Salad

### Makes 4 servings

**C**ouscous is made from semolina. It's a wonderful substitute for rice because it is already cooked; the only preparation is to soak the couscous in boiling water or chicken broth.

> **2 cups couscous, prepared according to package directions**
> **½ cup chopped grilled plum tomatoes (page 303)**
> **¼ cup chopped celery**
> **¼ cup chopped red onion**
> **2 tablespoons toasted pine nuts (page 303)**
> **2 tablespoons raisins**
> **1 teaspoon chopped fresh mint**
> **¼ cup olive oil**
> **2 tablespoons fresh lemon juice**
> **1 tablespoon honey**
> **½ teaspoon Tabasco**
> **Pinch ground cinnamon**
> **Salt and pepper to taste**

*Gather 'Round the Grill*

**P**lace the prepared couscous in a serving bowl and add the tomatoes, celery, red onion, pine nuts, raisins, and mint. In a small bowl combine the olive oil, lemon juice, honey, Tabasco, cinnamon, salt, and pepper and blend well. Pour the dressing over the couscous and toss gently. Chill 30 minutes before serving.

# Fruit Parcels

**Makes 4 servings**

Grill
*temperature*
**high**

**U**nited Parcel drivers aren't the only people who deliver packages. As these summer fruits bake in foil "parcels," the fruit steams and becomes soft, and the juices all blend together. Make sure you're home when this parcel arrives.

**1 cup large melon cubes**

**1 banana, cut into 2-inch pieces**

**2 peaches, pitted and quartered**

**1 cup small fruit such as strawberries, raspberries, or diced kiwi**

**1 cup seedless grapes**

**¼ cup brown sugar**

**2 tablespoons butter**

**1 teaspoon ground cinnamon**

**1 teaspoon chopped fresh mint**

**Whipped cream or ice cream**

**P**reheat the grill.

**I**n a medium bowl combine the melon, banana, peaches, berries, grapes, and brown sugar and mix well. Arrange evenly in the center of four 12-by-12-inch squares of heavy-duty aluminum foil. Dot with the butter and sprinkle with cinnamon and mint. Bring the 4 corners of the foil together and twist securely. Place the packets on high heat for 8 to 10 minutes. Serve with fresh whipped cream or ice cream.

*Holidays*
*Menu 28*

# Menu 29
## Father's Day

*Gorgonzola Mushrooms*

*Lobster Salad*

*Eggplant Parmigiana*

*Stuffed Veal Chops*

*Berries with Champagne Sauce*

Father's Day was first celebrated on June 19, 1910, in Spokane, Washington, where the local YMCA and the Ministerial Association persuaded the city fathers to set aside a day to "honor thy father." It was the inspiration of Mrs. John Bruce Dodd, who at age twenty-eight, wanted her father, William Smart, acknowledged because he raised six children alone after the death of his young wife. The only problem that might arise from serving this menu to Dad on the third Sunday of June is keeping him away from the grill.

# Gorgonzola Mushrooms

### Makes 4 servings

*Grill temperature*

**high, then medium**

**W**hen I grilled these mushrooms during a cooking tour in Germany, everyone lined up for seconds; unfortunately, I had cooked only enough for firsts, so be sure you don't make the same mistake. As a variation, add one of the following to the stuffing: ¼ cup grilled and diced ham; meat from 2 grilled spicy Italian sausages; or ½ cup chopped grilled shrimp.

**8 large mushrooms, 2 to 2½ inches in diameter**

**2 tablespoons olive oil**

**½ cup chopped grilled onion (page 303)**

**3 scallions, grilled (page 303) and chopped**

**Puree from 4 cloves Caramelized Garlic (page 302)**

**2½ cups fresh bread crumbs**

**¼ cup milk**

**1 tablespoon chopped fresh cilantro**

**½ teaspoon Tabasco**

**4 ounces Gorgonzola cheese, crumbled**

**P**reheat the grill.

*Gather 'Round the Grill*

**R**emove the mushroom stems with a knife and set aside. Brush the caps with oil, grill over high for 1 minute on each side, and remove. Chop the stems and combine with the onion, scallions, and garlic in a medium bowl. Add 2 cups of the bread crumbs, milk, cilantro, and Tabasco and mix well. Add the cheese and stir until the mixture is smooth. Fill the mushrooms caps evenly with the mixture and roll them in the remaining bread crumbs. Brush lightly with the remaining olive oil and grill over medium heat until tender.

# Lobster Salad

**Makes 4 servings**

For the want of another name, this dish is called lobster salad, but lobster is only part of the story. The chunks of grilled lobster are joined with shrimp, scallops, smoked fish, and the unexpected grilled melon. The dressing with just a hint of mint brings all the flavors together.

**Two 1½-pound lobsters, split in half lengthwise**

**Olive oil**

**½ pound large shrimp, peeled and deveined**

**½ pound sea scallops**

**1 large honeydew or casaba melon, peeled, seeded, and sliced**

**½ pound smoked fish, such as salmon, tuna, mako, or a combination**

**2 cups mixed salad greens, such as radicchio, endive, and arugula**

**¼ cup Lobster Dressing (recipe follows)**

Preheat the grill.

Lightly brush the lobsters with olive oil and grill, split side down, over high heat for 2 to 3 minutes. Turn the lobster over and cook 5 to 6 minutes longer at the cooler grill edges. Cool slightly, remove meat, and cut into chunks.

Lightly brush the shrimp with olive oil and grill over medium heat 5 to 6 minutes total, turning once.

Lightly brush the scallops with olive oil and grill over medium heat 4 to 5 minutes total, turning once. Slice each scallop in half horizontally.

*(continued)*

Lightly brush the melon slices with olive oil and sear on grill for a minute or so.

Arrange the lobster, shrimp, scallops, melon slices, and smoked fish on salad greens. Pour dressing over ingredients just before serving.

## Lobster Dressing

**Makes about ¼ cup**

**4 tablespoons olive oil**

**2 tablespoons balsamic vinegar**

**1 tablespoon Dijon mustard**

**1 teaspoon chopped fresh mint**

**Puree from 4 cloves Caramelized Garlic (page 302)**

**Freshly ground black pepper to taste**

Combine all the ingredients in a small bowl and mix well.

# Eggplant Parmigiana

**Makes 4 servings**

Eggplant Parmigiana is not typically a grilled dish, but many people asked me for some new and different ways to cook eggplant. They were tired of brushing eggplant slices with olive oil and throwing them on the grill.

*Grill temperature*

**high, then medium**

2 small eggplants, peeled and thinly sliced lengthwise

½ cup olive oil

2 cups Grilled Tomato Sauce (page 290) or your favorite tomato sauce

1 cup shredded mozzarella

¼ cup grated Parmesan cheese

Preheat the grill.

Brush the eggplant slices with olive oil and grill quickly on both sides. Layer the eggplant in an ovenproof baking dish or shallow casserole alternating with the sauce, mozzarella, and Parmesan cheese and repeating the layers until they're used up. Bake the dish for 20 to 25 minutes in a covered grill. Remove the dish and let sit for 5 minutes before cutting.

*Holidays Menu 29*

# Stuffed Veal Chops

### Makes 4 servings

**I**f you can't find veal chops in your market, buy pork chops because the stuffing goes equally as well with either. Sprinkling the cooked meat with lemon is a Sicilian custom adopted from Arab conquerors.

¼ cup chopped grilled eggplant (page 303)

2 thin slices prosciutto, finely chopped

2 tablespoons finely chopped mozzarella

1 tablespoon bread crumbs

4 veal rib chops, 1 inch thick, with a pocket cut in

Puree from 4 cloves Caramelized Garlic (page 302)

2 tablespoons finely chopped fresh sage leaves

1 tablespoon olive oil

½ teaspoon balsamic vinegar

1 lemon, cut into wedges

**T**o make the stuffing, combine the eggplant, prosciutto, mozzarella, and bread crumbs in a small bowl and mix well. Carefully fill each chop with a quarter of the stuffing and secure with toothpicks.

**I**n a small bowl combine the garlic, sage, olive oil, and balsamic vinegar and mix well. Coat the chops with this mixture and marinate 30 minutes in the refrigerator.

**P**reheat the grill.

**P**lace the chops on high heat and cook 3 to 4 minutes on each side for rare; 4 to 5 minutes on each side for medium. Serve with fresh lemon.

**V**ariations:
  Substitute wild mushrooms for the eggplant.
  Substitute smoked sausage for the prosciutto.

# *Berries with Champagne Sauce*

**Makes 4 servings**

1 cup orange juice

1 tablespoon granulated sugar

1 tablespoon cornstarch

1 cup berries (strawberries, blueberries, raspberries)

1 cup champagne

1 tablespoon brown sugar

*Grill temperature*

**high, then medium**

**P**reheat the grill.

**I**n a small saucepan, combine the orange juice, granulated sugar, and cornstarch. Bring the mixture to a boil, lower heat, and simmer 2 minutes. Remove the saucepan from the heat and add the berries, champagne, and brown sugar.

*Holidays Menu 29*

# Menu 30
## Thanksgiving

New England Clam Chowder

Ribs and Tomato Kraut

Brussels Sprouts and Pepperoni

Water-Smoked Turkey Tenderloins

Sweet Potatoes and Apples

Pumpkin Crème Brûlée

Thanksgiving is the one holiday during the year when the focus is definitely on food. Oh, yes, the Pilgrims and the parade are important, but the emphasis is the turkey and all the trimmings. Several generations meet at the table, from little tots to great-grandma. As we bow our heads in prayer before the feast, we reflect on the bounty of the harvest and on our family, and give thanks by joining together in prayer and food.

# New England Clam Chowder

**Makes 6 to 8 servings**

**H**ere's a version of a popular non-tomato clam chowder made with whole clams. Any type of firm white fish, such as cod, haddock, pollack, or halibut, can be added or even substituted for the clams. The soup will taste even better if the fish is grilled before it goes into the pot.

½ **cup finely chopped bacon**

**1 large onion, thickly sliced, grilled (page 303), and diced**

**2 ribs celery, diced**

½ **cup diced grilled scallions (page 303)**

**4 cups clam juice or fish bouillon**

**4 cups half-and-half**

**2 large potatoes, peeled and diced**

**1 tablespoon chopped fresh Italian parsley**

**1 teaspoon dried thyme**

**2 bay leaves**

½ **teaspoon Tabasco**

**24 littleneck clams, well scrubbed**

**2 red bell peppers, grilled (page 302), seeded, and cut into 1-inch pieces**

**Oyster crackers**

**P**reheat the grill or side burner.

**P**lace the bacon, onion, celery, and scallions in a 4-quart pot and cook over low heat for 2 to 3 minutes, taking care not to add color to the vegetables. Add the clam juice, half-and-half, potatoes, parsley, thyme, bay leaves, and Tabasco. Raise heat to bring soup to a boil, then lower heat and simmer 15 minutes, stirring occasionally. Add the clams and simmer 5 to 10 minutes, or until the clams open. Stir in the red bell pepper. Discard bay leaves. Serve with oyster crackers.

# Ribs and Tomato Kraut

**Makes 4 servings**

It's never Thanksgiving in Baltimore unless there's sauerkraut on the table. It doesn't seem to make much difference which way ribs are cooked; they're everyone's favorite. Make sure you have plenty of napkins ready for this one.

**3 pounds pork spareribs**

**¼ cup Herb Pork Rub (recipe follows)**

**2 medium onions, thickly sliced and grilled (page 303)**

**8 plum tomatoes, cut in half lengthwise and grilled (page 303)**

**2 cups fresh sauerkraut, washed and well drained**

**1 teaspoon caraway seeds**

**2 bay leaves**

Rub the pork on all sides with the herb rub and refrigerate 24 hours.

Preheat the grill.

Grill the ribs over medium heat for 8 to 10 minutes on each side. In an ovenproof dish combine the onions, tomatoes, sauerkraut, caraway seeds, and bay leaves. Bury the ribs in the mixture, cover, and place over medium-low heat for 30 minutes with the grill hood down. Remove the ribs and sear over high heat for 2 minutes. Discard the bay leaves. Serve the ribs on a bed of the tomato kraut.

*(continued)*

*Grill temperature*

**medium, medium-low, high**

*Holidays Menu 30*

# Herb Pork Rub

**Makes about ³/₄ cup**

¼ cup sweet paprika

3 tablespoons dried thyme

3 tablespoons dried rosemary

2 tablespoons garlic powder

1 tablespoon dried parsley

1 tablespoon fresh sage, or 1 teaspoon ground

½ teaspoon ground black pepper

½ teaspoon ground nutmeg

¼ teaspoon cayenne pepper

Combine all the ingredients in a small bowl and mix well.

# Brussels Sprouts and Pepperoni

**Makes 4 servings**

*Grill
temperature*
**high**

This may seem like an unusual combination, but the saltiness of the pepperoni and the cabbage flavor of the Brussels sprouts come together very well.

> ½-pound pepperoni stick, thickly sliced on an angle
>
> 1 tablespoon olive oil
>
> 1 pint Brussels sprouts, washed and trimmed
>
> 1 tablespoon honey
>
> ½ small onion, thickly sliced, grilled (page 303), and diced
>
> ½ teaspoon dried oregano
>
> Freshly ground black pepper

Preheat the grill.

Grill the pepperoni slices until slightly charred. Heat the oil in a sauté pan on the grill, toss in the Brussels sprouts and honey, and quickly stir-fry. Add the onion and oregano. Add the pepperoni to the pan and toss well. Sprinkle with black pepper and serve immediately.

# Water-Smoked Turkey Tenderloins

### Makes 8 servings

*Grill Temperature*

---

**indirect cooking**

**T**hese turkey tenderloins taste wonderful with a spicy mustard. Make an extra batch of the seasoning mix for the freezer and you'll have it ready for next time you feel like lighting the smoker.

**One 12-ounce bottle of beer**

**2 cups hot water**

**Trimmings from onion, celery, and carrot**

**2 bay leaves**

**¼ cup paprika**

**¼ cup dried parsley**

**¼ cup dried sage**

**1 teaspoon ground nutmeg**

**1 teaspoon dried basil**

**1 teaspoon coarsely ground black pepper**

**½ teaspoon garlic powder**

**8 to 10 turkey tenderloins (about 4 to 5 pounds total)**

*Gather 'Round the Grill*

**P**repare a charcoal smoker 40 minutes prior to smoking the tenderloins. Place the beer, water, vegetable trimmings, and bay leaves in the water pan.

**I**n a small bowl mix the paprika, parsley, sage, nutmeg, basil, black pepper, and garlic powder. Season the turkey tenderloins on all sides with the herb mixture.

**P**lace the tenderloins on the smoker rack, close the smoker, and smoke at 195° to 200° F. for 2 hours. Internal temperature should be 160° F.

# Sweet Potatoes and Apples

**Makes 4 servings**

When I was growing up, one dish I could be sure my mother would prepare for our Thanksgiving table was sweet potatoes and apples. Somehow the sweetness of the apples never overwhelmed the flavor of the sweet potatoes, and the sugar and spices made them both taste better.

*Grill temperature*
**medium**

- **4 large sweet potatoes**
- **4 eating apples, such as Golden Delicious or McIntosh**
- **¼ cup (½ stick) butter, cut in small pieces**
- **¼ cup light or dark brown sugar**
- **¼ cup granulated sugar**
- **2 tablespoons honey**
- **1 teaspoon ground cinnamon**
- **Pinch ground nutmeg**
- **¼ cup orange juice**

Preheat the grill.

Bake the sweet potatoes on the grill for 30 to 35 minutes or parboil, peel, and cut into thin slices. Grill the apples for 10 minutes, or smoke them for 20 minutes, then core, peel, and slice them into rings.

Layer the sweet potatoes and apples in a shallow buttered casserole. Evenly top with the butter, brown sugar, granulated sugar, honey, cinnamon, and nutmeg. Pour the orange juice evenly over the ingredients, cover, and bake with the hood down until the sweet potatoes are tender, 20 to 25 minutes.

*Holidays Menu 30*

# Pumpkin Crème Brûlée

**Makes eight 4-inch tarts**

**H**ere's an alternative to the traditional slice of pumpkin pie. If you feel squeamish about using a propane torch to caramelize the topping, run the tarts under the broiler for 30 to 60 seconds. Either way the crisp crunch of the topping contrasts with the creamy pumpkin custard.

1½ cups milk

1½ cups heavy cream

1 cup pumpkin puree, fresh or canned

1 teaspoon orange zest

½ teaspoon vanilla extract

8 egg yolks

¼ cup light brown sugar

¼ cup granulated sugar

1 tablespoon light corn syrup

½ teaspoon ground cinnamon

Pinch ground nutmeg

Pinch ground allspice

### For the Brûlée Sugar

3 tablespoons granulated sugar

3 tablespoons light brown sugar

½ teaspoon ground cinnamon

**P**reheat the grill or side burner.

**I**n a medium saucepan, combine the milk, cream, pumpkin puree, orange zest, and vanilla and bring to a boil, stirring constantly, then remove from heat.

**I**n the top of a double boiler combine the egg yolks, brown sugar, granulated sugar, corn syrup, cinnamon, nutmeg, and allspice and cook until the mixture is lemon-colored and coats a spoon, about 4 to 5 minutes. Slowly add the pumpkin mixture and continue cooking until the mixture has the consistency of thick custard, about 3 to 4 minutes. Remove the pan from the heat and pour into eight 4-ounce ramekins or tart shells. Chill 5 to 6 hours.

**I**n a small bowl combine the sugars and cinnamon for the topping. Just before serving, top each custard with 1 tablespoon of the sugar mixture. Light a propane torch and move the flame back and forth over the sugar until it darkens. Do not overheat or the custard will melt. (If using the broiler, watch carefully so the custards don't burn.)

*Holidays*
*Menu 30*

# Menu 31
## New Year's Day

*Antipasto with Garlic Oil*

*Fillet of Beef with Horseradish Sauce*

*Tuscan Artichoke Pie*

*Grilled Lasagna*

*Broccoli Rabe*

*Ricotta Pie*

**N**o sooner have we finished the Thanksgiving turkey than it's time to light the candles for Hanukkah and Christmas. It's snow, it's Santa, and it's spiritual. It's the holiday time leading up to New Year's, when we visit friends and invite them to our homes. Entertaining can be lavish or cozy, but if you really want to surprise your guests, serve them a totally unexpected grilled meal. And if you like Italian food, you'll love this menu. Let the festivities begin.

# Antipasto with Garlic Oil

### Makes 4 servings

Grill temperature

**high-medium**

**S**erved with a sharp cheese such as provolone and smoked meat such as prosciutto or salami, this vegetable combination could become a whole meal.

**3 red or green bell peppers, or a combination**

**2 to 3 medium red onions**

**1 medium eggplant**

**1 medium green or yellow squash**

**6 plum tomatoes**

**¼ cup olive oil**

**Puree from 1 head Caramelized Garlic (page 302)**

**3 to 4 basil leaves, finely chopped**

**2 tablespoons balsamic vinegar**

**Freshly ground black pepper to taste**

**P**reheat the grill.

**R**emove the seeds from the peppers and cut into ¾-inch-wide strips. Slice the onions ¼ inch thick. Slice the eggplant ⅛ inch thick on the diagonal. Slice the squash ¼ inch wide on the diagonal. Brush the peppers, onions, eggplant, squash, and tomatoes with 2 tablespoons of the olive oil and grill 3 to 4 minutes or until the vegetables are slightly charred. Turn and continue grilling until tender. Arrange the vegetables on a platter and drizzle with remaining olive oil, garlic, basil, and pepper.

# Fillet of Beef with Horseradish Sauce

## Makes 8 to 10 servings

Beef fillet is the boneless tenderloin, which is extremely tender. It is always cooked quickly and never eaten well done. Fillet is expensive, especially around the holidays, so find one on sale, buy it, and freeze it. You'll be glad you did. If that jar of horseradish in the refrigerator is more than a few months old, it's time to buy a new one.

**8- to 10-pound beef tenderloin**
**1 tablespoon Tabasco**
**Beef Rub (recipe follows)**
**¼ cup olive oil**
**Horseradish Sauce (recipe follows)**

Trim all the fat from the tenderloin and slice off the silver skin. Fold the thin end under so the tenderloin is the same thickness on both ends. Tie the tenderloin with butcher's twine every 2 to 3 inches (or have your butcher do it). Rub the meat with the Tabasco and dry rub and refrigerate for 24 hours.

Preheat the grill.

Thread the beef with a long skewer from a rotisserie and secure with the forks. Place the meat on the grill and baste with olive oil. Cook 35 to 40 minutes or until desired doneness. Remove and let the meat rest 10 minutes before slicing. Serve with Horseradish Sauce.

*(continued)*

*Grill temperature*
**medium**

*Holidays Menu 31*

# Beef Rub

### Makes almost ¹/₂ cup

2 tablespoons sweet paprika

1 tablespoon garlic powder

1 tablespoon coarsely ground black pepper

1 tablespoon dried thyme

1 tablespoon dried basil

1 tablespoon dried parsley

¹/₄ teaspoon nutmeg

Combine all the ingredients in a small bowl and mix well.

# Horseradish Sauce

### Makes about 1¹/₂ cups

¹/₂ cup mayonnaise

¹/₂ cup sour cream

1 tablespoon well-drained horseradish, or to taste

1 tablespoon Dijon mustard

1 tablespoon chopped fresh chives

¹/₂ teaspoon Tabasco

Freshly ground black pepper to taste

Combine all ingredients in a small bowl and mix well.

# Tuscan Artichoke Pie

### Makes 4 servings

This crustless quiche can be eaten warm or at room temperature and makes a tasty first course.

- **4 small artichokes**
- **Juice of 1 lemon**
- **¼ cup all-purpose flour**
- **1 cup olive oil**
- **½ grilled red pepper (page 302), cut into strips**
- **¼ cup grated fontina or sharp Swiss cheese**
- **3 tablespoons grated Parmesan cheese**
- **5 eggs, well beaten**
- **3 tablespoons half-and-half**
- **Puree from 4 cloves Caramelized Garlic (page 302)**
- **1 teaspoon dried oregano**
- **½ teaspoon Tabasco**
- **Pinch ground nutmeg**

Cut off the artichoke stems and remove all the tough outer leaves. Place the artichokes on their sides, and using a sharp knife, cut off the top ¼ inch. With kitchen shears, cut ¼ inch off the top of each leaf. Scrape out the choke with a teaspoon and cut the artichokes horizontally into thin slices. Place the slices in a medium bowl with the lemon juice and water to cover; soak for 5 to 10 minutes.

Preheat the grill.

(continued)

Drain the artichoke slices and dredge in flour. Quickly dip the slices in olive oil, place on the hot grill, and grill over high heat for 2 to 3 minutes, then turn and grill for 2 to 3 additional minutes. Cut the slices into small pieces.

Place the artichokes slices in a shallow buttered baking dish. Cover evenly with the red pepper strips, fontina, and Parmesan cheese. In a separate bowl combine the eggs, half-and-half, garlic, oregano, Tabasco, and nutmeg and mix well. Pour the mixture over the artichokes and grill over medium heat with the grill hood down until the mixture sets, about 12 to 15 minutes.

# Grilled Lasagna

**Makes 4 to 6 servings**

*Grill temperature*

**medium**

Lasagna is as American as apple pie or hamburgers and it's a fine addition to a holiday menu because it's a dish that everyone enjoys. This extra special version contains pine nuts and raisins.

- **1 pound ground pork**
- **1 pound ground veal or beef**
- **½ pound bread crumbs**
- **¼ cup grilled and chopped onion**
- **Puree from 3 cloves Caramelized Garlic (page 302)**
- **1 egg, lightly beaten**
- **2 tablespoons pine nuts**

2 tablespoons grated Parmesan cheese

2 tablespoons raisins

1 teaspoon dried oregano

1 teaspoon dried basil

Salt and pepper to taste

1 pound lasagna noodles, broken into 3- to 4-inch pieces

2 tablespoons olive oil

2 to 3 cups Grilled Tomato Sauce (recipe follows)

8 ounces ricotta

8 ounces mozzarella, thinly sliced

In a medium bowl quickly combine the pork, veal, bread crumbs, onion, garlic, egg, pine nuts, Parmesan cheese, raisins, oregano, basil, and salt and pepper to taste and mix well so that the ingredients stay well chilled. Shape the mixture into 10 patties and refrigerate for 30 minutes.

Preheat the grill.

Grill the patties over medium heat until the internal temperature reads 160° F.

Meanwhile, cook the lasagna until al dente. Drain well, place in a serving bowl, and toss with the 2 tablespoons olive oil.

Make 2 or 3 layers of the grilled patties, lasagna noodles, tomato sauce, ricotta, and mozzarella in a buttered shallow ovenproof 3-quart baking pan and serve immediately or place on grill, lower hood, and grill for 20 minutes over medium heat.

*(continued)*

*Holidays*
*Menu 31*

# Grilled Tomato Sauce

**Makes about 8 cups**

*Grill temperature*

**high, then low**

**T**his basic tomato sauce can be used on seafood, meats, vegetables, and of course, on pasta. Grilling the tomatoes give the sauce a hint of smoke and intensifies the tomato flavor.

> **4 pounds vine-ripened tomatoes**
> **¼ cup olive oil**
> **Puree from 1 head Caramelized Garlic (page 302)**
> **6 basil leaves**
> **Freshly ground black pepper**

**P**reheat the grill.

**W**ash the tomatoes and cut in half through the stem end. Place the halves on a very hot grill for 3 to 4 minutes on each side. Remove and place in a saucepan with the olive oil, garlic, basil, and pepper. Simmer the sauce for 30 minutes and run through a food mill.

# Broccoli Rabe

**Makes 4 servings**

Grill
*temperature*

**high**

First cousin of cabbage and turnip, broccoli rabe has green stalks and broccoli-like buds that have a pungent, bitter flavor. It's fast becoming a favorite of those who like its unique taste, especially when combined with lots of garlic. Broccoli rabe is especially delicious served over pasta.

**1 bunch broccoli rabe**

**5 tablespoons olive oil**

**1 lemon, thinly sliced**

**Puree from 1 head Caramelized Garlic (page 302)**

**4 to 5 chili peppers, grilled (page 303), peeled, seeded, and cut into**
   **½-inch pieces**

**Shaved Parmesan cheese to taste**

**Freshly ground black pepper to taste**

Wash the broccoli rabe in water and peel the stems if they are very thick. Place the rabe in 2 quarts boiling water and cook 4 to 5 minutes. Drain and toss with 2 tablespoons of the olive oil.

Preheat the grill.

Brush the lemon slices with the 1 tablespoon olive oil and grill 2 minutes on each side. Place the broccoli rabe directly on the hot grill and turn quickly. In a medium bowl combine the grilled broccoli rabe, lemon slices, garlic, and chili peppers and toss gently. Top with shaved Parmesan cheese and black pepper. Drizzle the remaining 2 tablespoons of olive oil on top.

*Holidays
Menu 31*

# Ricotta Pie

### Makes 6 to 8 servings

*Grill temperature*

**medium**

**I**f you make the ricotta pie several days in advance, the flavor will only improve as the holidays approach.

One 15-ounce container ricotta, drained

¼ cup granulated sugar

2 teaspoons chopped candied fruit

3 egg yolks

2 tablespoons all-purpose flour

1 cup heavy cream

1 teaspoon vanilla extract

1 tablespoon rum or anisette

Pastry for a 9-inch pie, prebaked for 8 to 10 minutes

Confectioners' sugar

**P**reheat the grill.

**I**n a medium bowl combine the ricotta, sugar, and candied fruit. In a small dish combine the egg yolks and flour and beat well. In a medium saucepan bring the cream to a boil. Add a little hot cream to the egg yolks, mix well, and return to the saucepan. Heat until the mixture thickens and has a pudding-like consistency, about 5 minutes. Stir in the vanilla, rum, and the ricotta mixture. Mix well and pour into the pie shell. If your grill has a shelf, place the pie pan on the shelf; if it doesn't, place 2 bricks side by side in the center of the grid and place the pie pan on top. Lower the grill hood and bake 25 minutes or until the filling pulls back slightly from the pastry. Cool 2 hours, then sprinkle with confectioners' sugar.

*Gather 'Round the Grill*

# Menu 32
## Patriotic Holidays

*Lamburgers*

*Hamburger Loaf*

*Smoked Chicken Legs*

*Chopped Grilled Salad*

*Apple Pie*

On the days we celebrate what it means to live in this country and be an American, we cook simple foods. But that doesn't mean the foods have to be frankfurters and potato salad (unless they're grilled, of course). This spinoff of a typical American backyard menu can be prepared on Presidents' Day, Memorial Day, Fourth of July, or Labor Day. Raise the flag and strike up the band!

# Lamburgers

## Makes 4 servings

*Grill temperature*

**medium**

**I**f you don't see ground lamb in your supermarket or butcher shop, by all means ask for it. Whenever you're mixing any ground meat product, it's a good idea to have the meat and bowl well chilled. Not only will a chilled bowl cut down on bacterial growth but it will help bind the meat. So, if possible, use a metal bowl for mixing the ingredients and place it in the freezer beforehand. If your kitchen is warm, place the bowl over a bowl of ice when you're incorporating the meat with the spices.

Don't even think of serving these or any burgers rare. According to the U.S. Department of Agriculture, all ground meats should be cooked until the internal temperature is 160° F. The patties can also be wrapped with precooked bacon before going on to the grill.

**2 pounds ground lamb**

**2 eggs**

**¼ cup chopped scallions**

**Puree from 4 cloves Caramelized Garlic (page 302)**

**2 tablespoons chopped walnuts or pine nuts**

**1 tablespoon finely chopped fresh Italian parsley**

**½ teaspoon Tabasco**

**¼ teaspoon ground nutmeg**

**Salt and pepper to taste**

*Gather 'Round the Grill*

**P**reheat the grill.

Combine the lamb, eggs, scallions, garlic, walnuts, parsley, Tabasco, nutmeg, salt, and pepper in a chilled bowl and mix gently but well. Form the mixture into 4 patties and grill for 4 to 5 minutes for well done.

# Hamburger Loaf

**Makes 4 servings**

Whenever a recipe calls for ground meat, make sure it's ice cold and work quickly. Don't leave the mixture sitting around, especially when it's combined with eggs.

*Grill temperature*
**medium-high, then medium**

1 cup crumbled day-old bread

¼ cup milk

8 ounces ground beef round

8 ounces ground pork

1 cup tomato sauce

1 medium onion, thickly sliced, grilled (page 303), and chopped

1 egg

Puree from 4 cloves Caramelized Garlic (page 302)

1 teaspoon dried basil

1 teaspoon dried oregano

Salt and pepper to taste

Hamburger Loaf Glaze (recipe follows)

Soak the bread in the milk for 5 minutes and squeeze dry.

*Holidays Menu 32*

*(continued)*

In a large bowl mix the beef and pork with a large fork until well combined. Add the bread, tomato sauce, onion, egg, garlic, basil, oregano, salt, and pepper and mix well.

Take two 14-by-24-inch sheets of heavy-duty aluminum foil and place one on top of the other. Place the meat mixture in the center and form into a loaf shape. Wrap the foil tightly around the meat and chill in the refrigerator for 1 hour.

Preheat the grill.

Place the foil-wrapped loaf on the grill over medium-high heat for 40 minutes, turning it several times. Remove the loaf and let it rest 5 minutes while you turn grill to medium. Carefully unseal the package and, without removing the foil, return the meat to the hot grill. Baste the meat with the glaze, lower the grill hood, and grill until the meat is a golden color, about 10 minutes.

## Hamburger Loaf Glaze

**Makes 1 cup**

**½ cup prepared mustard**
**½ cup catsup**
**2 tablespoons honey**

In a small bowl combine the ingredients and mix until well blended.

# Smoked Chicken Legs

### Makes 4 servings

*Grill Temperature*

**indirect cooking**

**I**f using a water smoker, fill the water pan with beer and some vegetable peelings. Presoak hickory or mesquite chips in water 30 minutes before adding them to the smoker box. With the smoker going anyway, cook a few extra chicken legs and freeze them for later use in pastas and salads and to eat alone with a chunk of bread.

> **8 whole chicken legs**
> **¼ cup Chicken Spice Rub (recipe follows)**
> **2 teaspoons Tabasco**
> **Chicken Dipping Sauce (recipe follows)**

**T**wenty-four hours before smoking, rub the chicken legs with the spice rub and Tabasco and refrigerate.

**P**repare smoker 30 minutes before smoking.

**P**lace the chicken legs on the smoker grate, close the cover, and smoke for approximately 2½ hours or until meat is done. The meat will shrink away from the leg bone and will pull toward the thigh. Another way to test for doneness is to turn the leg skin side down and prick it with a fork in the joint between the leg and thigh. The juices should run clear with no trace of red. This is important because smoking will leave meat pink in color. Serve with the dipping sauce.

*(continued)*

*Holidays
Menu 32*

# Chicken Spice Rub

**Makes about ¹/₂ cup**

¼ cup paprika

1 tablespoon dried thyme

1 tablespoon dried rosemary

1 tablespoon freshly ground black pepper

1 tablespoon granulated sugar

1 teaspoon garlic powder

1 teaspoon ground cinnamon

**I**n a small bowl combine all the ingredients and mix well.

# Chicken Dipping Sauce

**Makes about ¹/₂ cup**

¼ cup hoisin sauce

2 tablespoons catsup

1 teaspoon Oriental sesame oil

½ teaspoon Tabasco

½ teaspoon dry mustard

**C**ombine all the ingredients in a small bowl and mix well.

# Chopped Grilled Salad

### Makes 4 to 6 servings

A chopped salad is just that—all the vegetables are chopped into tiny pieces so that with every mouthful you get to taste all the ingredients. The best part of this salad is that you can use whatever is freshest from your garden or from the market.

**2 to 3 plum tomatoes, halved, grilled (page 303), and chopped**

**½ medium red onion, sliced, grilled (page 303), and chopped**

**1 red or yellow bell pepper, grilled (page 302), seeded, and chopped**

**1 small zucchini, grilled (page 303) and chopped**

**½ cup chopped peeled cucumber**

**½ cup chopped carrot**

**Puree from 4 cloves Caramelized Garlic (page 302)**

**¼ cup olive oil**

**3 tablespoons cider vinegar**

**1 teaspoon chopped fresh cilantro**

**½ teaspoon Tabasco**

**2 cups chopped mixed salad greens**

**½ cup croutons**

Combine the tomatoes, onion, bell pepper, zucchini, cucumber, carrot, and garlic in a medium bowl and toss gently. In a separate bowl mix the olive oil, vinegar, cilantro, and Tabasco. Pour the dressing over the vegetables and marinate 1 hour. Arrange the salad greens on a serving platter and top with the vegetables. Scatter the croutons over the vegetables.

*Holidays
Menu 32*

# Apple Pie

## Makes 6 to 8 servings

*Grill temperature*

---

**low-medium**

**B**efore the days of real ovens, cakes and pies were often baked in Dutch ovens over hot coals. This dessert is prepared in cowboy style.

> **4 to 5 apples, halved, cored, grilled (page 305), peeled, and sliced (about 3 cups)**
> **½ cup dried fruit (pears, peaches, etc.) or raisins**
> **½ cup light or dark brown sugar**
> **¼ cup molasses**
> **¼ cup dry bread crumbs**
> **1 teaspoon ground cinnamon**
> **½ teaspoon salt**
> **¼ teaspoon ground nutmeg**
> **½ cup melted margarine**
> **Biscuit recipe from Biscuits and Honey (page 201)**

**P**repare a charcoal or hardwood fire.

**I**n a large bowl combine the apples, dried fruit, brown sugar, molasses, bread crumbs, cinnamon, salt, nutmeg, and 4 tablespoons margarine and mix well.

**P**reheat a Dutch oven and grease the bottom with 2 tablespoons margarine. Line the bottom with half the biscuit dough and cover with the apple mixture. Cover with the remaining biscuit dough and brush with the remaining 2 tablespoons margarine. Cover the Dutch oven and nestle the pot in the hot coals, placing some of the hot coals on the lid. Bake for 20 to 25 minutes, or until the dough is light brown. Do not remove the cover until after 20 minutes.

*Gather 'Round the Grill*

Basics

# Caramelized Garlic

*Grill Temperature*

**low**

**G**arlic contains a lot of natural sugars, and when it's grilled these sugars caramelize and make garlic taste even better. Put a few extra heads on the grill and store them in the refrigerator; they'll keep for several days.

> **6 heads fresh garlic**
> **¼ cup olive oil**
> **One 12-inch square aluminum foil**

**P**reheat the grill.

**L**ay each head of garlic on its side and, using a sharp knife, cut ¼ inch off the bottom or root end. Brush the garlic with the oil and place on the cooler edge of the grill for about 20 to 30 minutes. Cover the garlic with the foil and continue grilling until the cloves are soft and creamy, another 20 to 30 minutes.

**T**o use the garlic, separate the cloves and squeeze out the garlic puree. The garlic can be wrapped and stored in the refrigerated for up to 1 week.

# Grilled Vegetables

*Gather 'Round the Grill*

**I**f you like your vegetables lightly colored and slightly crunchy, grill them for the shorter of the cooking times given here. If you like them charred, grill them an extra minute or two.

**Bell peppers:** Cut the peppers in half and remove stems and seeds. Brush lightly with olive oil and grill over high heat for 2 to 3 minutes on each side.

**Chili peppers:** Brush with olive oil and grill over high heat until charred, 2 to 3 minutes on each side depending on size.

**Corn:** Remove husk, brush with olive oil, and grill over medium-high heat for 15 to 20 minutes, turning occasionally.

**Eggplant:** Cut diagonally into slices, brush lightly with olive oil, and grill at medium-high 2 to 3 minutes on each side. If you want the eggplant peeled, remove the skin after it's grilled.

**Mushrooms:** Wipe with a damp paper towel or rinse quickly under cool water and pat dry. Brush lightly with olive oil and grill over medium-high heat for 4 to 5 minutes; move to the cooler edges of grill and cook until tender, 6 to 8 minutes longer.

**Onions:** Cut horizontally into thick slices, brush lightly with olive oil, and grill over high heat until tender, 3 to 4 minutes on each side.

**Plum tomatoes:** Cut the tomatoes horizontally through the stem end. Brush lightly with olive oil and grill over high heat until slightly charred, 2 to 3 minutes per side.

**Potatoes:** Wash and rub with vegetable oil. Individually wrap in aluminum foil and grill over medium-high heat. After 35 to 40 minutes, a sharp knife inserted in the center should come out easily.

**Scallions:** Brush lightly with olive oil and grill over medium-high heat until tender, 4 to 5 minutes, turning frequently.

**Zucchini:** Cut on the diagonal and brush lightly with olive oil. Grill over high heat for 2 to 3 minutes on each side.

# Toasted Nuts and Seeds

To toast 1 cup nuts or seeds, melt 1 tablespoon butter or margarine in a small skillet on the grill. Add the nuts or seeds and cook over low heat, shaking the pan frequently, until the nuts or seeds turn light brown, about 5 minutes.

# Pizza Dough

**Makes 3 to 4 pizza discs**

**I**f you want to try your hand at making pizza dough, be sure you allow enough time. The dough is refrigerated several hours for the flavor to develop.

Many supermarkets now carry fresh or frozen pizza dough, or perhaps your favorite pizzeria will sell you a pound or two if you don't have time to prepare it yourself.

**1 cup warm water (around 110° F.)**
**1 teaspoon active dry yeast**
**1 teaspoon sugar**
**3½ cups all-purpose flour**
**¼ teaspoon salt**
**2 tablespoons olive oil**

**P**our ¼ cup warm water into the bowl of a heavy-duty electric mixer and stir in the yeast and sugar. Set aside for 5 minutes to dissolve. Add the remaining ¾ cup water and stir well. Add 3 cups of the flour, the salt, and 1 tablespoon olive oil and mix until well blended. Set the dough hook in place and knead 7 to 9 minutes, adding the remaining ½ cup of flour as needed.

**G**ather the dough into a ball and cut into 3 or 4 even pieces. Roll each into a ball, place in a greased bowl, and let rise for 45 to 60 minutes or until doubled in size. Brush the dough with the remaining 1 tablespoon olive oil, cover with plastic wrap, and refrigerate 2 to 4 hours. Flatten dough into a 6-inch disc.

# Grilled Fruit

**Apples:** Core the apples and cut in half or crosswise into thick slices. (Peeling the fruit is optional.) Brush lightly with melted butter and grill over medium heat for 4 to 5 minutes on each side.

**Lemons:** Cut the lemon into thin slices, brush with olive oil, and grill over medium-high for 2 to 3 minutes on each side.

**Peaches:** Cut in half and remove pit. Lightly brush with melted butter and grill at medium-high 2 to 3 minutes on each side.

**Pears:** Cut in half and remove seeds. Brush lightly with melted butter and grill at medium-high 2 to 3 minutes on each side.

**Pineapple:** Cut horizontally into ½-inch slices. Lightly brush with melted butter and grill at medium-high 4 to 5 minutes on each side.

**Plums:** Cut in half and remove pit. Lightly brush with melted butter and grill at medium-high 2 to 3 minutes on each side.

# Grilled Meats

**Chicken livers:** Trim off any fat, brush with olive oil, and grill over medium heat for 10 to 15 minutes. They should be slightly pink inside.

**Ham:** Brush a ½- to ¾-inch ham slice lightly with olive oil and grill over medium heat for 4 to 5 minutes on each side.

**Sausages:** Prick sausages on both sides with a fork or sharp paring knife to allow fat to drain off. Place on a lightly greased grill and cook at medium-high for 20 to 45 minutes, depending on thickness.

*Basics*

# Index

*Index*

**307**

*Index*

*Index*

sausage *(continued)*
   *holiday stuffing, 254*
   *jambalaya, 244–245*
   *mixed grill and vegetables,*
     *54–55*
   *Portuguese bean soup, 16–17*
   *-stuffed potatoes, 144*
*scallions, grilled, 303*
*scallops:*
   *with broccoli and penne,*
     *grilled sea, 38–39*
   *lobster salad, 267–268*
   *seafood salad, 18-19*
*seeds and nuts, toasted, 303*
*shellfish, see specific shellfish*
shrimp:
   grilled papaya salad with Maui
     onion vinaigrette and, 172–
     173
   lobster salad, 267–268
   salad, grilled, 110
   seafood salad, 18–19
   with tomato pesto, 197
soup:
   beer cheese, 180
   chilled avocado, 145
   corn and white bean, 155–156
   country peanut butter, 188
   crab chowder, 84–85
   cucumber and yogurt, 29
   escarole, 42
   grilled tomato-basil, 258–259
   New England clam chowder,
     274–275
   onion bisque, 108–109
   Portuguese bean, 16–17
   Sonoran cheese, 118–119
   split pea, 217–218
spaghetti with zucchini and
   yellow squash, 196–197
spinach:
   chicken Florentine, 45–46
   grouper with orange on a bed
     of fresh, 95–96
   tomato pesto, 198
squash, yellow:
   antipasto with garlic oil, 284
   spaghetti with zucchini and,
     196–197

squid:
   fried calamari, 50
   linguine with, 162
   Louie's stuffed calamari, 90
   seafood salad, 18–19
steak:
   and beer, grilled sirloin, 183
   chicken-fried, 191
   chili-rub flank, with corn salsa,
     103–104
   dressing, 164
   New York strip, with
     mushrooms, 20–21
   salad, 163
strawberries:
   with champagne sauce, 271
   crepes with grilled fruit, 22–23
   fruit parcels, 263
stuffing, holiday, 254
sweet potato(es):
   and apples, 279
   cottage fries, 199
   and pecan calzone, 193–194
Swiss chard and pears, 85
swordfish:
   ceviche-style, on skewers, 146
   with olive relish, 30

tomato(es):
   antipasto with garlic oil, 284
   basil soup, grilled, 258–259
   cabbage sauce, 207
   chopped grilled salad, 299
   corn salsa, 104
   eggplant and olives, 251
   eggplant Parmigiana, 269
   five-alarm chili, 72–73
   grilled salsa, 143
   jambalaya, 244–245
   mixed grill and vegetables,
     54–45
   and okra, 192–193
   pesto, 198
   piquant, 201
   plum, grilled, 303
   and ribs kraut, 275
   sauce, grilled, 290
   vinaigrette, new potatoes with
     roasted, 46–47

tuna:
   lobster salad, 267–268
   marinade, 44
   Niçoise salad, 43

veal:
   breast of, 253
   chops, stuffed, 270–271
   grilled lasagna, 288–289
   shanks, barbecued, 228–229
vegetable(s):
   chips with beer cheese dip,
     76–77
   grilled, 302–303
   marinade, 55
   and mixed grill, 54–55
   New England smoked dinner,
     219
   *see also specific vegetables*
vinaigrette:
   grilled chicken, 93
   grilling, 111
   Maui onion, 174
   roasted tomato, new potatoes
     with, 46–47

water, New England beef
   smoker, 221
watercress, grilled chicken with,
   92
watermelon, pickled, 124
water-smoked turkey
   tenderloins, 278
wine and melon, 255

yogurt:
   and cucumber soup,
     29
   or mayonnaise garlic dip,
     51

zucchini:
   chopped grilled salad, 299
   grilled, 303
   mixed grill and vegetables,
     54–55
   pappardelle of, 127
   spaghetti with yellow squash
     and, 196–197

*Index*

**310**